A JOURNEY INTO FAITH

(The *Shlepp* From Moses To Jesus)

by

Martin Fromm

ISBN: 0-615-12222-1

Printed in the United States by Morris Publishing
3212 East Highway 30
Kearney, NE 68847
1-800-650-7888

DEDICATION

This book is dedicated to Clara Rubin, who has been one of the most profoundly influential people in my life. Clara has been a *Yiddisha* mama to many, but most of all to me. Her love and faithfulness through many years of difficulty, and even deprivation, made me realize that a relationship with God is real and viable.

From the time of our first meeting, before I came to faith, Clara never let me forget what it is to be a Jew, and the importance of teaching scripture from that frame of reference. I thank God for having accorded me the privilege of knowing this woman. She has been a good friend, a teacher who led by example, and an insightful individual who emphasized, above all else, that the mission field is where you stand.

ACKNOWLEDGEMENTS

I gratefully acknowledge my wife Judy, Raymond and Lee Cohen and so many others, too numerous to mention, who stood by me and encouraged me to teach the Word of God. Thanks as well to Stephanie Jacobs for the hours of help provided in getting these thoughts down on paper.

PREFACE

I have not broken any vows for a long time. I swore that I would never believe in Jesus. That vow was broken in 1968. I swore that I would never speak in public, which includes teaching or preaching the Word of God. That vow was broken as well in 1968, immediately following my coming to faith in Israel's Messiah. The next vow took a little bit longer to break, but within the year I was baptized in the name of the Father, Son and Holy Spirit. To the best of my recollection, no further vows were broken for the next thirty-one years.

I'm not quite sure in my mind if I did indeed break a vow, but I was adamant in my intention not to write a book. In any event, I did publish a book that serves as a reference in supporting the Messiahship of Jesus. This book, For Unto Us A Son Is Given, uses the Old Testament to establish the credentials of Jesus as Israel's promised Messiah. It also provides insights into typical Jewish arguments as to why it is deemed un-Jewish to believe in Jesus. The book attempts to counter every one of these arguments with appropriate scriptural responses without relying upon New Testament passages which are not generally accepted in Jewish circles.

After writing this book, a number of people expressed interest in finding out how I came to devote so much of my time and energy to support what I so passionately despised prior to my salvation experience. I was quite adamant in my intent not to include details about my personal experiences. If you are reading this it is obvious that, once again, I am straying from previous conviction. I hope, however, that this is the Lord's leading and not capriciousness.

Although personal testimonies are very much a part of Christian faith and tradition, I have never been overly impressed with what often seems to be emotionalism. Being very much a realist, I am more concerned with facts than feelings. Thus, my previous book undertook to provide evidence to reveal God's beautiful plan for humanity and prophetic fulfillment. I deemed it unimportant to include details of my personal convictions and how I broke with traditions that I held so dear. Yet, I continued to be bombarded by those who were intrigued with learning more about my personal testimony.

Don't get me wrong; I have never been reluctant to share some of the difficulties that hindered me from reaching my ultimate destination. On the other hand, I tried to be selective to help others understand that my intellect and not my emotions brought me to where I am today. Emotional testimonies can be somewhat suspect, and I refer to them as "testiphonies" in many instances. That is, the lives of those who share their witness do not always match their words. Further, as a rational, clear-thinking person, I realize that some of my experiences may seem far-fetched (if it were not for God's involvement). Since I have been admittedly skeptical regarding the claims of others, I worried that some of the unusual events in my journey to faith would be viewed as stemming from an active imagination.

Having said all this, and after giving due consideration to all objections, here I go. In response to frequently-asked questions, I'm committing to writing how a nice Jewish boy from the Bronx came to believe the unthinkable – Jesus is the Messiah promised in the *Tenach* (Hebrew scriptures)!

CONTENTS

1

THE JOURNEY BEGINS

Those of you who share my faith in Jesus presumably believe in the infallibility of scripture. As such, it is patently clear that Jesus fulfilled prophecy and satisfied all the biblical requirements to be recognized as Israel's Messiah. In general, gentile believers are not as familiar with the Hebrew scriptures (Old Testament) but, nonetheless, can relate to prophecy and fulfillment. Jewish believers who have a richer background in the Old Testament writings usually have an even greater appreciation of how Jesus filled the roles of substitutionary offering and *Goel* (kinsman redeemer). Unsaved Jews, however, do not see the connection, and perhaps this book will help you understand why they have so much difficulty relating to Jesus.

The more one reads the Bible, be he Jew or gentile, the more impressed he becomes with the scope of God's promises and the intricate details satisfied by Jesus alone. Every need in the heart of man is met, and we come to enjoy a most unique and personal relationship that continues to grow. In fact, we wonder how the truths that are now so obvious could not be seen previously. Who has not said, "I must have been blind not to see this before"? There were bones of contention which we now take for granted, and we must be reminded as per 1 Corinthians 2:14, "But the natural man receiveth not the things of the Spirit of God, for they are foolishness unto him; neither can he know them, because they are spiritually discerned."

Each of us was weighed down by baggage, preconceived ideas that interfered with our ability to bow the knee and humbly ask Jesus to take the reins of our hearts. (The American Heritage dictionary defines *shlepp* as "to carry clumsily or with difficulty". Thus, we use this word to describe my journey and the baggage I carried.) For the Jew, all of the usual stumbling blocks were magnified by anti-Semitic behavior not always recognized or understood by the non-Jew. Latent anti-Semitism still exists in the church today, and continues to have an adverse affect upon Jewish people. My personal journey to faith was particularly hindered by my inability to ignore the years of anti-Semitic acts I experienced in my youth.

Romans 1:16 represents one of the foundational reasons for the existence of the ministry with which I've been associated for more than thirty years: "For I am not ashamed of the gospel of Messiah, for it is the power of God unto salvation to everyone who believeth, to the Jew first and also the Greek, for therein is the righteousness of God revealed from faith to faith; as it is written, the just shall live by faith." In spite of this verse being part of God's Word, it is not only controversial, but a source of irritation to some who claim to be saved. Too many have bought into replacement theology, which promotes the understanding that the church has replaced Israel. Misapplying the premise that there is no difference between the Jew and the gentile, the notion became that God is through with Israel. The gospel, therefore, is no longer to the Jew first (and in some circles, not at all).

In one sentence we are told that the gospel is still the power of God unto salvation, and that the just are to live by faith. We do not have license to declare null and void any part of the complete thought. Since the gospel is God's power unto salvation, the divine order in reaching all remains unchanged. In essence, if we were to prepare a recipe that calls for eggs, milk and flour to be added in this specific order, we would not be inclined to object on the grounds that the flour is not inferior to the milk, and should be put in first. On the same basis it would be wrong to object that the Jew is not better than the gentile. He is first not by merit, but because the Master knows what order or recipe is to be followed to produce the best results. Presenting the gospel from a Jewish perspective reaches all, whereas ignoring the Hebrew scriptures and mindset greatly reduces the opportunity to reach the lost sheep of Israel.

Nominal Christianity has taught that the Jew is a "Christ-killer", and there are believers who have carried this teaching over to their present way of thinking. Jewish-Christian dialogue usually focuses on removing this stumbling block, but it is difficult to undo sins of the past. Various Roman Catholic popes and theologians have written treatises to avoid offending Jews by recanting these allegations, but no matter how many times the accusation is withdrawn or modified, church relations remain strained. In one breath the papal decree is not to hold Jews accountable for the death of Jesus, but contradictory statements subsequently stir up new strife.

Not long ago representatives of the PLO justified their belliger-ence towards Israel by pointing to the role played by Jews in the crucifixion. Jewish clerics were incensed that the pope remained silent when claims of deicide were raised anew. Papal spokespeople responded that their silence should not be viewed as agreement, but the silence was taken as tacit approval. The flames of mistrust continued to be fanned.

Equally controversial among Protestants and Catholics is the question of evangelization. Some denominations appear to be benevolent by not targeting Jews. Whereas this may be reassuring to Jewish people, it ignores the greater issue. Is the attempt to maintain rapport between the faiths more important than following the will of God? Dare we overlook the Word that reminds us that "faith cometh by hearing, and hearing by the word of God"? Paul raised this question in Romans 10:14: "How then shall they call on Him in whom they have not believed? And how shall they believe in Him of whom they have not heard; and how shall they hear without a preacher?"

Jews did not corner the market on being obstinate or taking exception to the preaching of the Word. If we stopped witnessing to those who take offense, no one would get saved. We must continue to reach out intelligently, in love and in conformance with God's plan. Perhaps we should look at the subject of anti-Semitism a little closer in order to understand how these attitudes evolved and how those of us of the Jewish faith have been conditioned to mistrust the motives of the evangelicals.

2

Anti-Semitism

God divides the world into two general categories: the Jew and the non-Jew, or gentile. All members of the remaining nations are, therefore, gentiles. No other division is required, since the Lord set Israel apart from the rest of the world, and His covenant was with them alone. Jesus came to the lost sheep of the house of Israel and recruited disciples who obviously were Hebrews, or Jews. Those who came out of mainstream Judaism did not in any way forsake their Jewish heritage. In fact, the basis for receiving Jesus was His credentials as the Messiah foretold in the scriptures. Clearly, He was the One of whom Moses and the prophets wrote.

Within the body of Judaism there were Pharisees, Sadducees and Essenes. These sects are comparable to the Orthodox and Conservative branches of the faith that exist today. However, a new sect evolved and became known as Christians (from the Greek equivalent of *Meshiach* [Messiah]). Christianity is now viewed as a religion separate and apart from, and diametrically opposed to, Judaism. We will explore some events that caused this perception to come about. For now, we should understand that those who call themselves Hebrew-Christians or Jewish-Christians might also be described as Messianic Jews. Within the definition of Messianic Jew there can be shades of difference, but that is not important to go into at this time.

It is recorded in Isaiah 49:6: "And He said, it is a light thing that Thou shouldest be my Servant to raise up the tribes of Jacob, and to restore the preserved of Israel: I will also give Thee for a light to the Gentiles, that Thou mayest be My salvation to the end of the earth." In accordance with God's plan, Jewish evangelists brought the salvation message to the nations, and indeed converts from this pagan background would increase and greatly outnumber the Jews who followed Jesus. The event that precipitated bringing the gospel to the gentile was the general rejection of Jesus by the majority of Jewish people. Thus, there was a split within Judaism and animosity arose between the traditionalists and this new sect. Jews persecuted Jews, and the feud was fueled by both political interests and religious differences.

Most of all, a frustrated race longed for complete fulfillment of prophecy, and that included the era of peace and the restoration of Israel to national prominence. The crucifixion of the alleged Savior was a disappointment to a nation seeking political sovereignty and provided a reason for most to forsake the hope that the Messiah had actually come.

With fewer Jews joining the ranks and increasing numbers of gentiles coming to faith, it would not be long before Christianity would take on a predominantly non-Jewish flavor. In fact, in order to appeal to the heathen element, a growing and permissive church allowed pagan rituals to be incorporated into the religious practices. It resulted in (among other things) Passover becoming Easter, Shavuos becoming Pentecost, and holidays like Christmas being observed without any true scriptural foundation. In some respects Christianity has strayed so far from the early roots of Judaism that at times it becomes barely recognizable.

During the early period of the church, when Judaism still played an active role, the Romans were in control of the land. They persecuted Jews and Jewish-Christians alike. A number of revolts against Roman tyranny resulted in more bloodshed and persecution. It drove an even wider rift between the traditional and messianic components of Judaism, since the followers of Jesus were not predisposed to go to war. When Bar Kochba led the second revolt, he was thought by many, including the influential Rabbi Akiva, to be the messiah. This, obviously, was not acceptable to the disciples of Jesus, and caused further alienation within the already-divided factions.

With the fall of Jerusalem and the destruction of the Temple, Jews were scattered and lacked unity. Gentile leadership within the Christian or Messianic faith had little regard for the Jewish heritage and was more inclined to embrace Greek philosophy. From that point forward, a number of influential spokespeople for Christianity were more and more blatantly anti-Semitic. Names revered to this day within the church, such as Justin Martyr, Ignatius, Origen and Jerome wrote and preached sermons that denigrated Judaism. The general thinking became that God was through with the Jew, and that the church replaced the Chosen People in God's eyes. It is extremely important to understand, however, that true fundamental Christianity never fostered this teaching, nor could such heresy be supported by holy writ.

It did not take some gentile Christians long before they placed the death of Jesus squarely upon the Jews. As this kind of inflammatory doctrine became entrenched within the church, it is no wonder that Jewish people, at best, disdain, and at worst, fear the teaching that promotes anti-Semitism. Within a few hundred years of this spreading paganism, a concerted effort was made to forcibly convert, expel and kill those who were in disagreement. Crusades were launched against the non-Christians, and both Jews and Moslems became fair game. During the period of the Spanish Inquisition there were Christian leaders tortured and murdered as heretics, and, for good measure, hundreds of thousands of Jews were slain as well. Often a choice was given to be baptized and renounce Judaism or to be burned alive and have one's property confiscated. Is it any wonder that many are amazed today when a Jew gets saved and claims Jesus as Savior? Just a short time before this most unfortunate chain of events, the marvel was that a *gentile* would claim faith in the Jewish Messiah!

The sixteenth century brought a number of reformers, members of the Catholic Church who raised objections to the false doctrines and pagan practices that had infiltrated the teaching of the church. Strong indictments were brought against papal improprieties, nepotism, the sale of indulgences and teaching salvation by works instead of the biblical doctrine of grace. One of the most vocal and best-known protesting voices (from which the term Protestant is derived) was that of Martin Luther. He even authored a tract: "That Christ Was Born A Jew". Luther was critical of the Catholic attitude towards the Jewish people, and was confident that the Jews would understand his desire to purge the apostate teaching and join with him in embracing the true faith.

The effects of anti-Semitism and abuse were not to be negated by the "suspect" actions taken by Luther. Outraged by this rejection, the Jews then became the object of his most vitriolic diatribes. The subsequent writings of Martin Luther were vicious and unfounded attacks and accusations against Judaism. He promoted not only the persecution of this new-found enemy, but called for the burning of their *torahs* (scripture scrolls), destruction of their synagogues, and even suggested that killing a Jew was doing God's service.

The Jewish people were not welcome in any part of Europe. They could either convert or be expelled, and one by one all nations forced them out. Later on Adolph Hitler drew from the material found in Luther's heinous treatises to validate and encourage the "final solution", the systematic slaughter of the members of this "inferior" nation. By the time the war ended and the holocaust survivors were liberated, one of every three Jews who was alive in 1939 was now gone.

I have taken the time to document some of the history of anti-Semitism to help the reader understand my mindset, as well as that of many of my contemporaries. Irreparable damage was done, and the Jewish folk of my generation harbor deeply-ingrained mistrust for the gentile in general and the Catholic Church in particular. In fact, as I think back, I had no idea what distinguished a Christian from a Catholic, and I am sure that a good portion of Jews still could not point out doctrinal differences. All non-Jews become lumped together, and although individually some can be accepted as friends, a guarded attitude remains against the majority. Even in the politically-correct society in which we live today where liberal attitudes justify and protect all other minority races and perverted lifestyles, anti-Semitic remarks are commonplace. Jew-bashing is fair game and is reflected in the traditional jokes about the large-nosed, money-hungry, power-seeking Zionists who are looking to take over the world.

The Irish-Catholic neighborhood of the Bronx where I grew up did nothing to instill in me respect or trust for the gentile. Unfortunately, there was deep-rooted bitterness in my heart, and if it were not for the love and power of Jesus, this never would have changed. My Jewish heritage has always been a source of pride, and those who denigrated what I held dear were not to be trusted. My parents taught me to respect all people and faiths. They reminded me as well that how I conducted myself would reflect not only on them, but upon all of Jewry. As the Chosen of God, we were held to a higher standard, and every Jew was his brother's keeper. I wish that all who profess to believe in Jesus would similarly understand how the actions of one brings shame and disgrace upon the multitude when fundamental Biblical teaching is ignored or compromised.

If being Jewish alone were not enough of a cross to bear, I was physically perfect as a target for the bullies of the world. My mother was a most excellent cook and encouraged me to enjoy her culinary efforts. As a result, I was known as the little, fat Jew-boy. My excess weight, by the way, was emphasized by my small stature. In fact, when I graduated from high school, I was the third shortest in the graduating class, barely five feet tall (I sometimes wonder how I turned out to be so well-adjusted, having been so tormented as a child . . . only kidding!).

My parents were not particularly tall, my father being about 5'9" and my mom just slightly over 5 feet. In looking back at a picture taken at my *Bar Mitzvah* (at the traditional age of thirteen), my mother was a full head taller than I. However, whereas I was a roly-poly, my dad was an outstanding physical specimen. He was quite handsome, in a rugged way, and since he drove a truck and did manual labor, he was very muscular. I was in awe of how he could bend a soda bottle cap with his nicotine-stained fingertips. His hands were so callused that he could light crumpled paper and simply extinguish the flames by clenching his fist, without feeling any effect of the fire.

Neither of my parents was well-educated. Dad had to bring his formal education to an abrupt halt without finishing high school in order to help support his family. My mom lost her mother at a very early age and never graduated from public school. This does not mean that they were not bright. My father spoke a number of languages, had an uncanny aptitude for math and wrote well. He was well-versed on many topics, politically aware and had an outstanding sense of humor to add to the balance. He was a strict disciplinarian, but he never struck us in anger. "Us" includes my older brother and twin sister.

My mother was the gentle, affectionate and more indulgent parent, but she never contradicted my father or sent mixed signals. In all the years that I have lived, I've never experienced a more loving and compatible relationship. My father worshipped my mother and was convinced that she was by far the most beautiful and thoughtful woman on God's green earth. Mom, in turn, considering her loss of parents so early in life, was married at seventeen and looked upon her husband as father, mother, friend and confidante. She loved and respected my father and brought us up to show the same respect. In short, I thank God to this day for the wonderful parents He provided.

Although neither was overly religious, they taught us to hold to traditional Jewish values and deemed it important that we have a proper Jewish education. My father brought us to the local *shul* (synagogue) to meet the orthodox rabbi who came from Israel. Dad was concerned that he would not have the financial means to put the three of us through Hebrew school. Rabbi Simcha Rabinowitz assured him that money would not be an obstacle, and that our education was of paramount importance, not the cost. Thus, the three of us attended *cheder* (Hebrew classes) and worship services in this little *shul*, approximately one-half mile from our home (a walk-up building without an elevator).

On the walk to classes and worship, which required my attending four times a week, I had to cope with the anti-Semites who labeled me as fair game for being Jewish. I was seen as an easy target due to my small stature. After all, fat little Jews don't run very fast, and due to my size are not too adept at self-defense. Snowballs were thrown in winter and rocks in summer. Frequently my tormentors would rip up my Hebrew books and take my *yarmulka* (skullcap). I was assaulted, punched and thrown to the ground regularly. How I longed to be bigger and better capable of defending myself! My brother had grown to six feet, and my twin sister was several inches taller than I was. Being a late bloomer, I didn't slim down and reach six feet until I was past twenty-one years of age.

One of the favorite games played by the more belligerent was to have a particularly small and younger lad accuse me of having called him a name, or hitting him. Then six or seven would come to his defense, each delivering a punch and a kick in punishment, while two of them kept my arms pinned behind me. There were times that I was bound hand and foot and dragged through the empty lot across the street from my house. My tormentors thought it was amusing when I cried and screamed in pain as the sand and rocks ripped my clothing and my flesh. The physical abuse extended to being stabbed in the stomach with a switch-blade knife, and I bear scars to this day on both my legs where I was thrown on to a spiked fence.

I found it difficult to understand how human beings could have so much hate and intolerance simply because I was born a Jew. Yet I was more determined than ever to stand up for my faith, and never to be ashamed of my heritage and culture. I was proud of the accomplishments of my people and made no secret as to my heritage. It embarrassed me that some Jewish people actually changed their names to avoid being identified with the rest of us. By contrast, I would never dream of removing the *mezuzah* (a small, hollow, precious-metal container which holds verses from Deuteronomy) that hung from a silver chain around my neck. Years later I received a gold chain to which I attached a beautiful interleaved gold *Mogen David*, or star of David. I still make it a practice not to remove the chain, even to shower or swim. Ironically, the unbelieving Jews cannot understand why someone who believes in Jesus would wear this Jewish symbol. This often opens the way to meaningful dialog.

The first thirteen years of my life were spent in this neighborhood, and it was a nightmare! When my brother was old enough to go to work and add to the family income, we moved. From the two-bedroom apartment where the three children shared a room, we went to a three-bedroom so that my sister could now have her privacy. The extra bedroom was icing on the cake; the real reason to rejoice was in leaving such unpleasant neighbors behind. Before closing that chapter of my life, I might add that I had two gentile friends who attended the Catholic church that served that section of the Bronx. According to them, the priests in their parish taught that Jewish Christ-killers deserved any mistreatment they got.

My new neighborhood in the Bronx had a higher percentage of Jewish people. There was more of a mix between Jewish and Italian, and these two cultures enjoy many similar values that promote compatibility. I was attending DeWitt Clinton High School where there were many other Jewish students. As a result, there was considerable abatement in the anti-Semitic attacks. While it didn't disappear completely, I was in a much more comfortable environment than that from which I had come. The trip to school required a half-hour ride on the elevated subway line, so not too many from the school became my close friends. In my later teens the scope of my outside relationships became even more limited since I was now dating, and starting to work evenings and weekends.

The rap on Jewish people has often been that they are clannish and want nothing to do with the *goyim* (gentiles). Frankly, our parents taught us that Jews dated Jews, and that it was a *shanda* (shame) for a Jewish boy to date a *shiksah* (gentile girl). A non-Jewish boy is a *sheigitz*. (My father would joke that the definition of a *sheigitz* is a guy who thinks a *shiksah* is an electric razor!) Be that as it may, Jewish upbringing to date within our own was not regarded as an indictment against other races. It was rather a safeguard against inter-marriage, which is forbidden on a Biblical basis. Let's not forget that the call to Abraham was a call to separation, and that this holds true for the believer, who is not to be unequally yoked with the unbeliever.

The subject of inter-faith marriage is most problematic in Jewish circles. Though commonplace today, that was not the case when I was growing up. The Holocaust had taken over six million lives, and our numbers had greatly diminished. Inter-faith dating leads to inter-faith marriages, and ultimately results in raising children with little or no training about their heritage. Many rabbis have concluded that one of the reasons for God allowing the Holocaust was punishment for the growing number of inter-marriages in violation of His will. Indifference towards inter-marriage results in diminishing Judaism and produces the same effect as the Holocaust. Thus I would never have dreamed of dating a young lady of a different faith, no matter how pleasant and attractive she might be.

3

Coping In A Gentile-Dominated Society

I hated school, but enjoyed working. After all, for the first time in my life I had a little money in my pocket. This was somewhat of a dilemma, as my father always emphasized the importance of an education. "Don't be stupid like me", my father would say, "Work with your head, and not your back. Get a good education." I would soon have to make a decision, for I had sufficient credits to graduate even though I was only seventeen. In spite of having such little regard for school, and even though I never studied or did homework, I had a retentive memory and managed to have acceptable grades. Due to my cavalier attitude, I was not aware of my potential, and did not regard an education as being nearly as important as did my father.

No one in the Fromm family up to now had ever graduated from college; not my parents, siblings or any uncles or cousins. The thought of my earning a degree was so remote. When I finally chose to attend the Bernard M. Baruch School of Business and Public Administration, it was meant to appease my father. I never dreamed that I would actually go on to graduate and be awarded the Bachelor of Business Administration degree I received years later. But once again, I'm getting a little ahead of myself.

Since I was not a diligent student to say the least, I had no idea that I could even get into college. The grades received in high school were alphabetical and not numeric, so I did not attach a quantified value as to where I stood in terms of academic achievement. I had fallen in with a crowd that had little enthusiasm for education, and we concentrated more on sports than grades. When the time came for graduation, I was sitting towards the back of the auditorium with my buddies, who were not exactly over-achievers. Those who distinguished themselves and were to receive awards were seated in the front rows where they had ready access to get up to the stage with minimum delay. Imagine my amazement when I was called up to receive the Hebrew award and the English award. Not only was I embarrassed that my fellow "jocks" found out that I wasn't just barely passing (as I led them to believe), but the ceremonies were delayed waiting for me to come all the way from the back to go on stage for the presentations.

I remained ambivalent about going to college, especially since I realized that my financial contribution to the family was important. This led to a compromise whereby I decided to attend the evening school division at Baruch while working during the day. Fortunately, this was economically feasible, since the City University required those with a grade average of ninety or above to pay only a token tuition. Since I never expected to continue to graduation, I justified attending by reasoning that it was not costing me much money. To my surprise, I was able to juggle going to college, working full-time during the day and holding on to a weekend job at a candy store where I was employed during high school.

Finding a full-time job was not too easy, as I was limited by my lack of education. In addition, many firms were not enthusiastic about hiring Jews. The prejudicial hiring practices were not overtly anti-Semitic, but the reaction of the interviewers to my being a Jew was obvious. The best I could hope for was a ground-floor position that required no special training or experience. Ultimately, I landed a job with a major insurance company as an errand boy in their mailroom. The starting pay was about eighty or ninety cents an hour. Fortunately, the hours were 8:30A.M. to 4:30P.M., so I was able to carry ten credits a semester in night school.

There were only a handful of Jews in the corporation that employed several thousand. My coworkers in the mailroom were totally void of ambition, and ridiculed me for taking the job so seriously. They would take their time, leisurely strolling through the city, engaged in girl-watching, while I ran as quickly as possible to complete each errand and return for my next assignment. Their cutting remarks didn't dissuade me, as I was brought up to be conscientious, and I was accustomed to being ridiculed. In the back of my mind was my father's exhortation that how I behaved would reflect upon all people of the Jewish faith. Consequently, I was determined to provide my boss with no reason to criticize the Jewish work ethic.

The supervisor of the mailroom was impressed with my dedication and hustle. Within a few months he gave me the opportunity to work in the mail-room duplicating department. I soon mastered using the folding and inserting equipment, and graduated to the addressograph and multilith machines. I disliked getting ink under my fingernails, and never felt that my hands were really clean. However, my desire to get ahead was enough motivation to keep me going. The others in this printing department were at least twenty to thirty years older than I happened to be, but I viewed this position as a bridge to making more money and a chance to show my adaptability. My contemporaries were more concerned with the social aspects of the job, but I was highly motivated to get ahead.

Within six or seven months my diligence paid off. The kindly supervisor of the mailroom made me his assistant. My salary climbed to forty-two dollars a week! This allowed me to give my mom about thirty dollars a week to help with the household expenses and left me with approximately eight dollars to cover my carfare, daily newspaper, lunches and dating. This small measure of success kept me motivated and confident that more opportunities would come along. The fact that I pushed myself and was openly looking for promotion, however, did not sit well with some co-workers who accused me of being a "pushy Jew".

I learned there was a subscriber relations department that was involved with responding to customer inquiries via telephone and letters. My supervisor gave me permission to speak to someone in the personnel department to inquire about the possibility of a transfer. During the interview some less-than-complimentary remarks were made about Jews, but I fought back my instincts to retaliate in kind. They tried to discourage me by claiming that only college graduates were hired for this department. I argued that I was presently attending college and that I had received the English award upon graduating from high school. Perhaps I wore down the personnel director, or maybe she expected me to self-destruct because I would not be able to keep up with the college graduates in the department. In any event, I was hired on a trial basis with the stern warning that if I failed, I would be let go.

It took me less than a year to be more productive than anyone else within the department. I was producing twenty to thirty percent more work, and received outstanding performance reviews whenever I was evaluated. Over the next couple of years there were openings for lead correspondent and for trainers. In spite of the fact that I was best qualified, I was passed over in every instance. The excuse to my face was that I was too young, but it was obvious that less-qualified "WASPS" were used to fill these openings.

I continued to apply myself, and was now earning about seventy dollars a week. Since my father had never earned more than one hundred dollars weekly, I thought that I was doing well. My expectations were limited because I never dreamed that it would be possible for me to earn more than my father had made at the height of his earning capacity.

At this point my career was interrupted by Uncle Sam. I received a draft notice, and, after passing the physical, I was sent to Fort Dix, New Jersey for processing. The first seventy-two hours spent in the Army involved minimal processing and maximum K.P. (kitchen police). Between peeling potatoes and scrubbing garbage cans, I had my fill of army life. My work ethic did not extend to the inanity of the military, and I found everything about the army to be distasteful. I did not want to dress like everybody else, be subject to the same rigid rules or be compelled to associate with the crude element surrounding me. The other recruits seemed to be illiterate, foul-mouthed, unhygienic and hostile to Jews. I resented having to eat, shower, work and go to the bathroom with a crowd, and among those for whom I had little respect. Living in a fishbowl is not exactly appealing to a person who relishes his privacy.

In order to have some respite and collect my thoughts, I went AWOL for a day. When I returned the barracks was empty, and I learned that all my fellow recruits had been shipped off to Fort Benning, Georgia for basic training. The platoon sergeant was furious that I missed the plane and understandably skeptical of my explanation that an officer sent me to police the parade grounds. I was well aware that recruits were often told to go to that area to pick up paper and debris, so this was a convenient excuse to cover for my mysterious disappearance. After all, I added, I was told never to question orders given by anyone holding a higher rank than I did. That included just about the whole world, and there was no way to prove that I was lying.

I was left at Fort Dix to take basic training with the next wave of newcomers. They were not much better than the previous lot, but I wasn't about to tempt fate by disappearing again. The only break I got during the following eight weeks was taking Friday nights and Saturdays off to observe the Jewish Sabbath. I used this opportunity to establish a rapport with the Jewish chaplain and convinced him to recommend that I attend chaplain assistant school. This was done to avoid being sent to advanced infantry training, rather than to satisfy any religious convictions.

I had my fill of crawling through the mud, firing rifles (which terrified me), sleeping in tents, going without bathing, climbing up and down ropes, etc. The food was intolerable, and there was no way that I could eat half the slop that was flung onto the greasy metal trays we had to use. Mushroom gravy spilling over to my Jell-O or ice cream was not particularly appetizing, and I could never get used to just about every entree being prepared with bacon or bacon grease. I was determined to find a way to avoid the regimentation and gung-ho mentality by getting into a training program that required use of one's brains rather than playing Tarzan or G.I. Joe.

Recruits with the highest aptitude test scores were given the opportunity to attend army administration school. This course was a prerequisite as well for attending chaplain assistant school. I asked to take the necessary tests and scored in the top percentile. As a result, I was called before a placement officer who indicated that I could attend the administrative classes. He explained that upon completion I would be required to sign up for Officer Candidate School. Since there was no other option, I gave my assent. Frankly, I never intended to sign the papers for officer training, as that would mean adding another year to my stay in the army. There was no way that I would extend the minimum two-year requirement by even five minutes!

The officer who authorized my attending the schools of my choice went ballistic when I later informed him that I changed my mind and had no desire to become an officer. In retaliation, even though I had been trained in a non-military specialty, he swore that I would be transferred to an infantry regiment that was leaving the next day. That night I disappeared and conveniently showed up after the plane took off. Naturally, I assured the puzzled cadre that I was following orders that I received from a superior to police the parade grounds.

I had no desire to go overseas, and hoped to finish my "hitch" stateside. More as a punishment than anything else, they sent me to Orleans, France where there was believed to be an opening for a Jewish chaplain's assistant. When I got there, however, I learned that the position was already filled. Within a few weeks I was reassigned to Poitiers, France, about 240 miles from Paris. The rabbi there was more down to earth, as he was not a career officer. He had no idea as to what I should be doing, so he pretty much allowed me to set my own routine. It was an easy life, but frustrating nonetheless. There were very few Jews on post, and I made only one friend with whom I had even the least bit in common.

My time was spent as liaison to the French Jewish community, which included the publishing of a newsletter to keep the Jewish personnel and French Jews aware of what was going on. I would write about the Jewish holidays and current events, and attempted to get the Jews interested in learning more about Jewish culture and tradition. It was an impossible task because the French hated the Jews. Few were willing to reveal their Jewish heritage in fear of reprisals from the Catholic community. There were frequent incidents of anti-Semitism which included breaking the store windows of Jewish merchants, painting swastikas, defacing synagogues, desecrating headstones at Jewish cemeteries, etc. The hateful acts perpetrated by the predominantly Catholic populace kept most of the Jews in hiding.

I never ate in the Mess Hall, and avoided as much as possible coming in contact with military personnel. Learning where inexpensive restaurants served edible food, I chose to eat off base and pretty much keep to myself. I was terribly homesick, and wrote to my mother and father at least once a week. Not wanting to upset them, I never revealed quite how miserable I was. Frankly, I wondered how I would survive my remaining year in the army without going out of my mind.

I had become friendly with the Red Cross representative on base who happened to be married to the Adjutant General. She was quite a few years older, but took a liking to me (on more than a platonic level). As a result, she would offer to take me to Paris on weekends when I could get a pass. I was not particularly attracted to her, but it was expedient insofar as getting away and having someone to pay the bills. I'm not particularly proud of taking advantage of this relationship, but it helped keep me sane and allowed lonely weekends to pass a little more quickly. It also afforded me the opportunity to see parts of France that I would never otherwise have been able to visit.

No diversions sufficiently compensated for the loneliness and emptiness I felt from being in an alien country among people who had such open hostility for Jews (and for Americans as well). I dreaded each new day, and longed for the time when my army career would come to an end. There was nothing more comforting than getting a letter from home, and I looked forward to the day that I would go back. Unfortunately, the precipitating circumstances that made this possible were devastating. One day the Red Cross volunteer worker came to tell me that my father had a fatal heart attack, and that I was cleared to go home for the funeral. It haunted me for years that in some mysterious way my father sacrificed his life to get me out of France and back to my family.

The days that followed were surreal. How could this be? My father was only fifty years old and a perfect physical specimen. The telegram I was given indicated that he was lighting a cigarette at work, fell to the ground, and was dead on the spot. He suffered a massive heart attack allegedly stemming from an enlarged heart. He had never been sick, worked a physically demanding job, and yet the autopsy revealed that he suffered from a congenital defect. Death had never hit so close to home, and to someone I held so dear. I couldn't control the tears that streamed down my face, and knew only that I had to get home to see my mother.

In those days jets were not readily available and the army used propeller flights that took a long time to cross the ocean. On the way over to France we stopped at Gander, Newfoundland and someplace in England in order to refuel. The return trip was even worse. There were a number of mechanical problems with the plane, in addition to the refueling delays. We stopped in Germany, England, Ireland and Harmon, Newfoundland. The trip took three days (including being stuck overnight in England waiting for a commercial flight). The delays seemed interminable, and I was constantly fighting back tears. The Jewish custom is to bury immediately, and within three days at the outside. Not only was I struggling with the concept of losing my father, but I was frantic that I wouldn't make it home in time for the funeral.

When I finally arrived in the Bronx, my family was just preparing to leave for the funeral home. There could be no more delay, and my mother reluctantly resigned herself to my not being there. I arrived home in the nick of time, and we were able to mourn together as a family, and to help comfort each other. As bad as it was for me and my siblings, I will never know how my mom survived such heartache. She was inconsolable and her tear-streaked face and reddened eyes have been etched into my memory. I knew that I was needed at home and initiated the process to obtain a hardship discharge on the basis of being the sole support of my mother. It took several months, but I was finally discharged.

Although I was back with my family, I couldn't shake the queasy feeling that the price that was paid was my father's life. He was my hero, and the feelings of loss were compounded by a sense of guilt. To add to these confused emotions, I had a burning need to be reassured of my father's love. He had never been particularly demonstrative, and would show an unusually soft side only when it came to my sister. She was his little girl, and somehow fathers could fondle a daughter, but not a son. I prayed for some kind of a sign that would provide the balm for my wounds.

It took over three months for my personal belongings to reach me following my return from France. In fact, I had all but forgotten about the clothes left overseas, including the uniforms and military paraphernalia that we received upon induction. When I finally went through my effects, I found a letter that my father had written the day before his death. This in itself was unusual, for he normally left the letter writing to my mother. Perhaps he would add a word or two at the end, but rarely wrote himself. This was different; not only did he write several pages, the crux of the letter was to let me know how much he loved me, and how proud he was to have me as a son. To this day I believe that my father had in some way come back from the grave to offer these words of comfort. They meant so much in the dark days when I missed him most. The fond memories remain, and what grieves me now is that he never had a chance to meet my wife and son (who, incidentally, is named after him).

After the mourning period, my older brother returned to his wife and family, and my sister soon left to continue her education in Florida. I returned to the insurance company where I was working before entering the army. I came home night after night to find my mother sitting in the dark and weeping. She had never held a job, so she had nothing to distract her or to occupy her time. I realize now that I would have been wiser to encourage my mother to go to work, but I mistakenly thought I could replace my father and take care of all her needs. She ultimately convinced me that she should work, and it proved to be therapeutic.

4

Life Goes On

I continued to work at the insurance company, and took on more responsibility. Before long I was in charge of three departments and became the highest-rated division chief in the company. In spite of this, raises in pay were minimal, and the Jewish resentment remained as an undercurrent to my employment. Although I was now responsible for approximately seventy-five people, I was only earning about ninety dollars a week. This was sufficient to take care of my needs, including paying the rent for the apartment that I shared with my mother. It had been almost a year since getting out of the service, and my days continued to be spent at work and my evenings at school where I resumed my education.

The depression over my father's death was dissipating, and my mother encouraged me to start dating again. It was just about this time that the woman I married, and have lived with for forty years, came into my life. After a relatively short time I knew that I wanted to marry her. When I discussed my feelings with my mother, she was very supportive. In fact, up to then I was not only paying all the bills, but I was in the habit of turning most of my paycheck over to her. Upon learning of my intentions to marry, my mother said that now I was to think of my future, and she refused to accept any more money from me.

My sister at this time was attending school in Miami, and my brother lived in Brooklyn with his wife and two young children. I was not particularly fond of his wife, and suspected that he wasn't happy. I was very partial to his son, and would make it a practice to pick him up on Saturday mornings while the rest of the family was still sleeping. We would take long walks together or go to the park or the beach, or just hang out. During the summers I would take my mom upstate to the Catskills, and, whenever possible, bring my nephew. Then one morning my brother told me that he couldn't live with his wife any longer. He moved in with my mother and me.

This didn't last very long, for one night my brother said that he intended to get a divorce. He was in love with someone else and was not going back to an unhappy marriage. I assured him that I supported any decision he would make, as long as he did the honorable thing in attending to his children. Obviously, my brother was not pleased with what I had to say, and when I awoke the next morning, he was gone. He packed up and disappeared during the night, and I didn't see him again for perhaps twelve years. The pain of losing my brother was compounded by the fact that my sister-in-law, understandably bitter at being forsaken, never allowed the members of our family to see the children again.

Shortly thereafter I got married. It was a very small wedding, as we did not have much of a family left. My wife had a small family as well. She had an older sister who was married with two children, and a third came along a little later. We would often babysit for our three nieces, and we grew very close to my sister and brother-in-law. They struggled considerably to meet their financial obligations, and often needed help from their parents. Later on in life they became extremely successful, and it is hard to imagine how difficult things had been when they first started out.

Life in general was pretty good, as I was now earning more than one hundred dollars weekly, and my wife made even a little more. However, we were now talking about starting a family, and planned to buy a house. I hoped that my boss would be able to pull some strings to get me some more money, especially since we had become good friends. He happened to be a homosexual, but he respected me because we could be open and honest with each other, in spite of the differences in our lifestyles. As much as he wanted to get me a raise, his hands were tied. Once again I learned that the company was unsympathetic to the "pushy Jew".

Under ordinary circumstances I would have quit, but my strategy was to be fully vested in the pension plan before leaving. Qualifying required a minimum of ten years of service and being a minimum of thirty years of age. I had almost eleven years of service, but was only twenty-eight. It was not in my best interest to walk out and lose well over twelve thousand dollars in pension money (which was a lot of money back then).

Having said this, it was just not meant to be. The icing on the cake resulted from a confrontation with a new administrator who was not only a blatant anti-Semite, but also had no appreciation for those of us who had been loyal to the company for many years. At one of our weekly supervisory meetings he shouted, "If anybody doesn't like the way I run things, I'll be glad to give him the *New York Times*" (to look for another job). Standing up in anger and frustration, I responded, "I'll take my copy now", and I left. Eleven years of my life went down the drain, with my pension.

The very next day I landed a job with a major manufacturer of Swiss watches assembled in the United States. They were glad to offer me one hundred fifty dollars a week to start, an increase of fifty percent over what I had been making! With the additional increases and bonuses I earned over the next two years, I more than made up for the loss sustained upon leaving the insurance company. Even more important, I was appreciated and was given an opportunity to hone my managerial skills. Best of all, I was now employed by a company founded by a Jewish family that had no problems with my religion.

Within a short time my wife and I moved into a three-bedroom house in Far Rockaway, and had a bouncing baby boy to fill one of those bedrooms. He brought a whole new dimension into our lives, and I never dreamed what a thrilling experience becoming a father would be. It meant a lot to me as well, to be able to name my son after the wonderful father I had lost. Needless to say, my mother shared this sense of gratitude, especially since she had lost contact with her firstborn's children.

Since then I have owned two other houses. I find this incredible, since I was convinced that only rich people owned homes. I never imagined that I could be a homeowner, and to this day I thank God for being so benevolent. Sometimes I look around my very modest home and marvel that by the grace of God I have so much more than I could ask or think. This probably makes little sense to those of you who grew up in better circumstances. By contrast, those of us who were raised in dingy neighborhoods and lived in four- or five-story walk-ups appreciate the difference. Buildings with elevators were a luxury that we could never afford. Other amenities now taken for granted were foreign to us as well. We didn't own a television set until I was in my teens, and the closest available phone was in the lobby of the building, not inside the apartment.

There may be others who will remember when most incoming phone calls were made to a local candy store. As kids we would hang around to answer the phone, and then race to let our neighbors know they had a call. Usually you would be rewarded with a penny or two for alerting them to the call. Those who enjoyed better circumstances, usually when the older children contributed money to the household, could then afford the luxury of a four-party, or if you were really riding high, a <u>two</u>-party telephone line. A private line was rare indeed in my old neighborhood.

Upon considering the material and emotional rewards that were now being reaped, especially when contrasted to the circumstances surrounding my childhood, I must repeat that life was good. As far as I knew, there wasn't much that I lacked. True, being somewhat materialistic I always wanted more, but at least I realized that I had come a long way. I was doing well on my job, my son was healthy and a delight, and we had good friends. What more could I ask for? I believed it couldn't get much better than this, but I never dreamed how much worse it could get. It was precisely at this time that a monkey wrench was thrown into the mix, and from a direction that I would never have expected. This brought us to a crucial turning point in our lives, as the subject of Jesus was introduced. As a child, Jesus was responsible for my misery, but now He was presented as my Savior. My inclination was to dismiss this absurdity with dispatch, but it wasn't as easy as might have been expected.

5

The *Shlepp* To Jesus Begins

In referring to my wife's sister and her husband, I did not mention that theirs was an interfaith marriage. This was a grief to my in-laws who, though not extremely observant Jews, found it all but impossible to break with traditions. Even more alarming was their obsession with what other people would think. As a consequence, when their firstborn started dating a young Italian man from a Catholic background, it was unthinkable. What would the rabbi say; what would the neighbors think? You can rest assured that they did all within their power to short-circuit this relationship.

My sister-in-law, Myra, was extremely assertive, strong-willed and rebellious, so nothing could be done to dissuade her. In fact, she may even have derived some satisfaction in knowing that her parents would be aggravated by her maintaining this relationship. In any event, to the consternation of her parents, and certainly without their blessing, the seventeen-year-old Jewish lass and her nineteen-year-old boyfriend eloped. My poor wife-to-be, then fourteen years old, was delegated the responsibility of breaking the news to Mama and Papa.

Fortunately, as time went on, the strained relations were repaired, and my brother-in-law, Ron, won everybody over. This is a tribute to his having been one of the most thoughtful, courteous and good-natured people that I had ever met. (Tragically, he passed away at a very young age, which was a great loss to us all.) He was easy-going, a considerate husband, doting father and a most decent human being. He often put the concerns of others above his own, and he was loved and admired by all. But, the early years of the marriage were stressful because Ron was not Jewish.

I have to admit that I do not personally approve of intermarriage, but would not look to impose my values upon others. My reservations about my brother-in-law had more to do with our being so completely different. I was ambitious, and he seemed to be too laid back. I was very liberal and he was by contrast a political and fiscal conservative. I read a lot, was more intellectually inclined, and my brother-in-law had only a high-school education. He had a lot of respect for the tenets of Judaism, but I had no respect for Catholicism. He may have been a nice guy, but not my type.

One weekend Myra and Ron went to a hotel in the Catskills. They were seated at a table with another couple who shared a similar background. The wife was Jewish and the husband an Italian who was raised in the Catholic Church. Since both couples were forced to cope with the problems of intermarriage, a conversation started as to how the children were being raised. The couple shared that they had no conflict with the differences in their background or in raising the children. They regarded themselves as Hebrew-Christians, in effect, embracing both faiths. They saw no contradiction in this, and proceeded to explain all about their strange Biblically-oriented religion.

As the weekend went on my sister-in-law and her husband were eager to learn more about their new friends and their faith. They were fascinated with this pleasant couple and enjoyed their companionship. Everything they were told made so much sense, and before the weekend was over, my sister-in-law invited Jesus to come into her heart. Myra was euphoric, and even though she had never previously exhibited concern about religious matters, she was thoroughly convinced that the time had come to change.

Upon returning from the weekend, Myra could not wait to let my wife know what had taken place. She was literally overflowing with joy and enthusiasm, and excitedly spoke of her spiritual awakening. Her younger sister, as ever, was influenced by Myra's persuasiveness, and that night she told me all that had taken place. My wife was mirroring some of the excitement seen in her sister, and she was convinced that this was something for us to check into. To the contrary, I was appalled!

I became so livid that I ranted and screamed about my wife's naivete and told her that I'd never explore something so stupid and heinous. I had no desire to learn about a hybrid faith that was probably some kind of ecumenical movement that compromised true Biblical teaching. After all, I spent my whole life defending my faith in the midst of persecution, and that was not to be in vain. On the other hand, my wife was always unduly influenced by her older sister, who was brain-washed. It struck me as incredible that my wife could not see how absurd and self-serving this new faith happened to be. Hebrew Christianity was tailor-made for interfaith couples who were used to compromise, not for those of us who understood true Judaism.

My wife tried to calm me down, but to no avail. She gave in to being out-shouted, but little did I know that this was not to be the end of this topic. Several days later Judy broached the subject again (as her sister continued to tell her about the exciting changes taking place in her life). Although I may have been less vitriolic, I insisted that the subject be dropped once and for all. To my chagrin, the pleading continued. My insistence that she demonstrate more concern and respect for our heritage did little to keep my wife from countering that I would be better served to find out more before jumping to conclusions. I should be more open to investigation, she insisted..

Once more I somewhat more calmly assured my wife that this was insanity. Her sister married out of the faith and needed a compromise; we didn't. Myra had three young girls to raise and they would need religious training that both she and her husband could live with. This was not a problem with which we had to cope. I tried to make Judy understand that what Hitler couldn't do through annihilation, and what the Crusaders could not accomplish through forcible conversion, was now being perpetrated with a most insidious and demonic movement. Screaming as loud as I could, I argued that if she were so intent upon satisfying her spirituality, she should learn more about her own religion. Our ancestors survived for five thousand years without Jesus, and we certainly didn't need Him now!

The High Holy Days of Rosh HaShannah and Yom Kippor were upon us, and I attended services at the synagogue without my wife. This only poured oil on the fire. She expected me to look into a ridiculously unscriptural religion, but did not care enough to come to temple to observe the faith of our ancestors. I could not understand how blind she was, and I resented Myra and Ron, who were responsible for driving this wedge between us. I didn't for one minute believe that they were evil or conniving, but I did believe that they were foolish and naive. How could any semi-intelligent and somewhat rational human being actually believe that Christianity and Judaism were compatible?

I sat down with Myra and Ron and tried to reason with them. Using every argument that could be mustered up, I assured them that they were being deluded. They had a need, and this pseudo-religion was a means of satisfying that need. It was wrong for them to try to influence others who had no reason to seek a compromise. The more animated and loud I grew, the calmer they remained. Their composure served only to make me angrier and more convinced that they had bought into a manufactured lie from the pit of hell.

My wife realized that I was not about to change my mind, so she tried a new tactic. Would I drive her to the home of a Jewish couple in Huntington Station, New York, where they hold Bible studies on Friday evenings? She wouldn't force me to sit in on the study; I was only to bring her there and back. Judy's wiles were pretty transparent, and I was not about to be sucked in, so I emphatically refused. My wife did not give up easily and repeated her request in subsequent weeks. Finally, she used the magic words that all wives use as a last resort: "If you really love me, you would." What could I possibly do but reluctantly agree to be her driver?

The following Friday evening we made the first of what proved to be countless trips to the home of Clara and Joe Rubin in Huntington Station, Long Island. I thought that my act of appeasement would soon satisfy my wife, and that within a week or two her strange flirtation with Christianity would come to an end. There was no doubt in my mind that I would quickly expose this movement as a farce, and life would return to normal. Who would have imagined that I would wind up teaching in this home for over twenty years, ending only when the Rubins retired to Deerfield Beach, Florida? But, once again, I'm getting ahead of myself.

At that time my wife and I were living in Far Rockaway, which is the southern tip of Queens County. Going to Huntington Station meant driving north to the Long Island Expressway, heading east to Huntington and then continuing further north. The trip requires going through Queens, Nassau County and into Suffolk County. With the weekend traffic, including those going out to the Hamptons and shore resorts, this trip would often take at least an hour and a half, if not two hours. Needless to say, the prospect of coping with all this traffic to attend a class teaching about Jesus was not high on my list of priorities. Consequently, when we finally arrived at the home of this apostate Jewish family, I was not exactly in a good frame of mind.

Joe Rubin was friendly, but somewhat reserved. His wife Clara was much more outgoing. It was soon obvious that Clara was the dominant figure in the marriage, and in everything else. She radiated enthusiasm, always had a broad smile on her face, and twinkling eyes that hinted of good humor and kindness. She was the typical "five-by-five", short and stocky and with a Buddha-like belly that heaved up and down with her laughter. She was the typical "bobba", or Jewish grandmother, wearing the traditional apron, short stockings or anklets instead of nylons, and glasses hanging from a string around her neck. Though we had never met before, Clara greeted me like a long-lost friend. She rushed over, grabbed me tightly, threw her arms around my neck and gave me a warm kiss on the cheek.

I was somewhat taken aback by such an elaborate demonstration from a stranger, but Clara didn't miss a beat. Before I could react, she was squeezing me all over and, in a stream of Yiddish, plying me with questions about my background. It was so disarming that I couldn't help but laugh and relax, in spite of myself. I wanted to hate the woman whose home was used to perpetuate the preaching of the gospel, but Clara made this impossible. Part of me remained wary while another part intruded upon my negative instincts. Perhaps good-natured Clara was duped along with all the other misguided Jews who bought into this preposterous religiosity.

The first thing I had to recognize was that Joe and Clara were actually Jewish. That is, I fully anticipated meeting nominal Jews who had no true sense of Jewish identity. I have met many such Jews for whom I had little tolerance. They either denied their heritage or lacked appropriate respect and understanding for our glorious culture. As far as I was concerned, too many Jews were shallow and lacking because they did not know, or care to know, about our history. My Jewishness was an important part of my sense of identity, and the teachings of Moses were the foundation of the greatest faith in the world. Those Jews who changed their names to avoid detection of their background were a disgrace.

Clara, on the other hand, was bursting with my brand of *Yiddishkeit* (Jewishness). Not only did she speak fluent Yiddish, she possessed the Jewish sense of humor that I adored. She could make outlandish statements and use words that might be considered crude and offensive in refined circles, but from her lips everything took on a different tone. In the ensuing years I learned that although Clara had a great love and concern for humanity in general, and the Jewish people in particular, her joviality and clownish ways were designed to disarm and put at ease all who crossed her threshold.

I was then introduced to the speaker, or Bible teacher, Raymond

Cohen, and his wife, Lee. Again, I was taken aback, since the name, Cohen, made it obvious that these were fellow-Jews, and not Christians who were promoting this ecumenical nonsense. Ray and Lee were pleasant enough, but certainly not nearly as exuberant as Clara. There was no hug and kiss, just a handshake and a smile. My initial reaction was distaste for this short, slightly-built man who epitomized in my mind what it is to be a self-hating Jew. When I responded to the introduction in Hebrew, the puzzled look on his face told me exactly what I suspected. He didn't even speak or understand the language of our ancestors, so how could he have the *chutzpah* (gall) to teach scripture?

As others who came for the study entered, I was introduced to each of them. There was a wide range of ages represented in the twenty or twenty-five in attendance. All were dressed casually, displayed warm smiles and were pleasant. Most, however, were not Jewish. Since the home was decorated with Jewish symbols, pictures with *Mogen Davids* (the star of David), *menorahs* (lamp stands), *torah* scrolls, scenes of Israel and pictures of rabbis, I could not fathom why the gentiles were attracted to this place. In subsequent visits I learned that all of those who attended identified closely with the Jewish people, and were grateful for the Messiah of this Chosen People Who died for their sin.

When everyone went downstairs to the finished basement that was set up like a classroom with folding chairs, I remained upstairs in the kitchen. After all, I had come only to drive my wife, and I was not about to subject myself to the insufferable teaching that was to follow. No coercing could convince me to join the others, so they ultimately left me alone. My practice to remain upstairs when the class was conducted continued for several weeks, but eventually I did join in.

Before the actual study Clara led the group in song. The words were written in phonetic Yiddish, but were praises to God, His Messiah and *Yeshua* (the Hebrew name of Jesus, equivalent to "Joshua", or "the Lord is salvation"). Some Jewish people may have found the use of the Hebrew name to be disarming, but I was not to be fooled by such a blatantly obvious device. Using the Hebrew, *Meshiach* or "Messiah" instead of "Christ", was also of no avail. Sugar-coated terminology was not to make the name of Jesus any sweeter. It was in that atrocious name that I was beaten and humiliated, and it was in that name that so many of our people were massacred during the Holocaust.

When Ray and Clara spoke of *Yeshua*, I used the term "*Yeshu*" as did many hostile Jews. Little did they realize that this was an acronym for *Yismach sh'mo v'zichri*, "May his name and memory be blotted out". The strains of the music and Yiddish singing in tribute to the Lord and His Messiah filtered upstairs, and it was difficult not to hum along. I may not have agreed with all the lyrics, but a good portion of the words and music were traditional Hebrew melodies and psalms. They were having a grand old time singing and praising God, but I could not help but feel that it was an affront to the God of Israel. It was even more disturbing that my wife was down there in their midst.

When the music ended, Raymond Cohen began the Bible study. He spoke well and displayed passion in getting his points across. He possessed an excellent vocabulary, and his thoughts were well-organized. There was no doubt that the audience related well to Ray. On the other hand, I listened intently while making mental notes to challenge a number of points that Ray made in his exposition on several Bible passages. I couldn't wait for the session to end, and I was eager to go on the attack when they came back upstairs. I was confident that I would be able to expose Ray for the fraud I thought him to be. The Christians, or Hebrew Christians, who attended would soon learn what it is to be a real Jew.

Clara put out coffee, tea, bagels and cake for all, and we gathered around the kitchen table to partake in the refreshments and conversation. Those who could not fit at the table brought up folding chairs and sat nearby. Most of the conversation centered around the excellence of the message they had just heard, and some made personal applications to the teaching. Not able to take it any longer, I began a barrage of attacks and questions that took everybody by surprise. How could someone abuse such fine hospitality, and even worse, challenge their beloved teacher? Only Ray remained calm and seemingly indifferent to my tirade.

I accused him of twisting holy writ and of having no knowledge of the original Hebrew or their nuances of meaning. Pointing out what I deemed to be misquotes, I demanded to know how much Ray was being paid to pervert true Biblical theology in order to corrupt the minds of the unsuspecting and naïve. (I learned that Ray's teaching was a labor of love, and that, to my great surprise, all this time and effort was donated without remuneration.) Sitting back with a smug look on my face, I dared Ray to respond. From the look on my wife's face and the stunned silence of the others, I thought I had won at least a partial victory.

Ray remained nonplussed while raising an eyebrow and asked simply, "Did you notice how many times you prefaced your remarks by 'I think'? Frankly, I don't care what you think." My face turned red and the blood was boiling in my veins. How can any sane and intelligent person profess not to care what I think? After all, my thoughts and intellect are of great value, and my background and training in Judaism by far exceeded his. How dare he suggest that my thoughts are irrelevant?

Before I could answer a word, Ray continued, "The only thing I am interested in is what the Word of God says. Everyone has an opinion, but the only thing that really matters is what is written in the Bible." Now every eye was on me, and I turned a brighter shade of red. I certainly had no idea where to find the Biblical passages to support my views. How embarrassing not to be able to back up my ranting with pertinent verses! Ray proceeded to turn to various portions of his very worn Bible to show me in black and white why he was able to make the statements he did. And for one of the few times in my life, I was speechless!

I couldn't wait to get out of there. My wife lingered, apparently enjoying the refreshments and the charming crowd. She particularly took a liking to Lee Cohen, and was not nearly as anxious as I was to call it an evening. When I finally convinced her to leave, I wanted to crawl out unnoticed, but Clara threw her arms around me, gave me a kiss, and invited me to come again. I thought that I surely would be back, but armed with enough Biblical references to overwhelm that evil man who was not easily rattled with my superior background. I left with the parting words that he was using a *goyish* (gentile) Bible to pervert and confuse the gullible, but the original Hebrew manuscripts would expose his lack of scholarship.

The subsequent weeks proved to be not too different from the first encounter. I waited upstairs making mental notes to challenge Ray, and then lashed into tirades to discredit his misleading commentary. Only this time I came prepared with my Isaac Leeser Hebrew and English text from the Hebrew Publishing Company. To my chagrin and amazement, however, Ray always knew where to find support for his exposition, even in my Bible. Although I would resort to claiming that he misunderstood the original Hebrew, the excuses I used were hollow and lacked conviction. I began to realize that my plan to expose Ray as a deceiver was not going to be nearly as easy as I had initially assumed.

There still was no doubt in my mind that Hebrew Christianity was a paradox in terms, and that this was truly a nefarious movement. Christianity was a tool of the devil, but it would take a greater effort on my part to prevail. My tactics began to change, and I knew that I had to talk less and listen more. It was also incumbent for me to learn more so that I would not be embarrassed when Ray pointed to obscure verses of which I knew nothing. Now I gathered a number of different Bibles, the King James, the Vulgate and others, so that I could make line-for-line comparisons to show where the contradictions existed. It was laborious and time-consuming, but well worth the effort to destroy the perverters of truth. (This is one more area where I was way off-base, and was shocked to see that although some words may be translated differently, all Bibles are basically the same in content.)

It was around this time that my wife and I sold our home in Far Rockaway and bought our first brand-new home in Nesconset, Long Island. This move brought us east of Huntington, and we now had to travel only twenty or twenty-five minutes to the Friday evening classes. By then I had grown more comfortable, and I even worked up the courage to sit downstairs during the Bible study. However, I still waited in the kitchen while they were singing praises to Jesus. I remained resolute in not allowing the worship of this alleged second Person of the triune God to corrupt my thinking. I even developed a greater tolerance for Ray and Lee Cohen, and respected Ray's patient demeanor and knowledge of scripture. It also dawned on me that he might even be sincere, but duped.

The trip to my office in the city from the nearby Smithtown station on the Long Island Railroad took almost two hours each way. That time was spent reading scripture. I attacked the word with eagerness and was experiencing great rewards. Not only was I learning so that I could better challenge the strange doctrine offered on Friday evenings, I was becoming so much more aware about the Biblical foundation of Judaism. This brought about the realization that I didn't know nearly as much as I had imagined, and my spiritual instincts were being revitalized. As the days wore on, fellow passengers would see me reading the Bible, which provoked many questions. Without fully realizing it, I was discussing the merits of Christianity and the claims of Jesus with neighbors and complete strangers. These deep philosophical and scriptural discussions became a daily routine and kept my juices flowing.

Before long, my wife didn't have to convince me to be her driver. I looked forward with anticipation to the Bible studies. Between these classes and my personal reading, I was growing in leaps and bounds. While I retained suspicions about the Jesus movement, I had to admit that the people who attended, including the gentiles, were the most loving, caring and decent human beings I had ever met. All my preconceived notions about vicious and contemptible Christians who accused me of being a Christ-killer were being mitigated by true Bible believers who respected Judaism and the Jew. Strangely, so many gentiles wore the Star of David to identify with the Jewish people, and expressed their gratitude for the Hebrew Messiah who grafted them into the stock of Israel. These people actually made it a practice to pray for the peace of Jerusalem and to share in love their faith in Israel's Savior.

My wife and I started to spend a lot of quality time with the Cohens. Not a day would go by that my wife and Lee didn't speak on the telephone at least once. We now saw Ray and Lee virtually every weekend, either Saturday or Sunday, in addition to the Friday night class. I actually began to like Ray, and was challenged by his spirituality. While I couldn't agree with many of his conclusions, I no longer questioned his sincerity and wisdom. Of course, spending more time with the Cohens also meant more quality time with the Rubins. Clara and I grew particularly close. To this day we have a special relationship which the fifteen hundred miles between New York and Florida cannot diminish.

Since Ray and Lee lived in Connecticut, and we spent so much time together, we often slept over at their house, or they spent the weekend at ours. While Judy and Lee did their thing, Ray and I would speak late into the evening exploring the wonders of God. It continued to bother me that Jesus couldn't be separated from the Bible, but I was being pulled in all the more. It was difficult not to see so many prophecies that appeared to point to Jesus. Is it possible that this could actually be true?

In my saner moments I was intransigent. I must have been missing something, and I would need outside help to deal with the dilemma. I started taking my wife to rabbis in the Long Island area to get their perspective. They would help me to straighten her out, and provide the missing pieces to the puzzle that I apparently overlooked. Convinced that I now would find a solution, I breathed a little easier. After all, I was brought up with the greatest respect for rabbinical authority and scholarship, and they would have the answers I wanted so badly to hear. I thought, may God forgive me for ever entertaining the notion, regardless of how briefly, that the Messiah we looked for could be Jesus. If there were any truth to this absurdity, the rabbis of old would have embraced Him, so there is no way that it was possible.

6

The Devil's Advocate

Visiting rabbis in the hope of finding support to challenge the Christian interpretation of scripture proved to be frustrating and somewhat disturbing. The great respect and admiration that I had for rabbinical intellect and scholarship was severely tested. To my amazement, I learned that I probably had a better knowledge of scripture than those I sought out. Their area of expertise was *Talmud* (the ancient rabbinical commentaries consisting of *Mishna* and *Gemmarra*, the basis of religious authority for traditional Judaism). Orthodox Judaism generally exalts *Talmud* and accords it equal status with *Torah*, based upon oral tradition.

None of the rabbis would commit to making an overt statement regarding the application of prophecy. That is, they would not venture an opinion when I referred them to messianic passages. They remained uncommitted and would open the *Talmud* to see what the great minds of the past had to say. It was clear that they were puzzled and incapable of offering a reasonable rebuttal, so they chose the safe course in relying upon what the classic interpretation happened to be.

When I attempted to point out the obvious flaws to the Talmudical interpretation, the rabbis became cool and often hostile. Several flew into a fit of rage and ordered me to leave their offices. It was astonishing that they had no desire to maintain the dialogue when challenged to justify commentaries that were clearly inconsistent and untenable in light of the context of the biblical passage under discussion. I had hoped to be shown my stupidity in opening myself up to Christian theology, but the intolerance displayed by the irate rabbis only aroused greater doubts as to the possible validity of Jesus' credentials.

There's an old joke about a Jewish man who was forcibly converted to Catholicism by a local priest. He attempted to call his wife, then his son and finally his daughter, to come to his aid. All three had flimsy excuses that kept them from coming in time to stop the conversion ceremony. The Jew then exclaimed, "I'm a Catholic for one minute, and already I hate three Jews." Well, I was far from being a

Catholic, or even a Christian, but I was harboring resentment that those I trusted to help me were so antagonistic to sincere inquiry and research. I wanted desperately to put this chapter of my life behind me, but I couldn't let the subject drop until I knew for sure that there was no merit to viewing Jesus as the Messiah of the Old Testament.

Perhaps, I reasoned, a new tactic should be employed. Jews have a penchant for winning souls back to faith when steps are being taken to convert. By openly challenging traditional Jewish thinking I led others to believe that I actually believed in Jesus. I figured that there would be a greater inclination to work for my redemption. Seeing me as a lost soul would be an incentive to steer me back to true Judaism. Thus, I played the devil's advocate and renewed my efforts to find fellow Jews who had *rachmonos* (pity) for my fallen condition. The results proved to be equally frustrating.

I would engage anyone in conversation who had the time and patience to listen. Not getting anywhere with the rabbis, I broached the subject with friends and neighbors. Since I attracted crowds on the Long Island Railroad by reading the Bible, I used these opportunities to discuss my alleged faith with all who came along. Group discussions would take place, and I had to defend my position with six or seven at a time. Being outnumbered changed nothing, and it was rare that I had much trouble stumping all who sought to prove me wrong. This may have been intellectually stimulating, but at the end of the day I still had to cope with the uncertainties that plagued me. Jesus was responsible for the persecution and death of so many of my people that I wanted to be able to hate Him and His false religion.

I would think back to my father and remember how he was willing to sacrifice so much to get his children a proper Jewish education. Was I desecrating his memory in this foolish pursuit? I reasoned as well that even if it <u>were</u> true, I could never bring myself to becoming a *goy* (non-Jew). It might be more prudent to stop searching than to reach a point of no return. Even if the end of the road brought me to such an unacceptable conclusion, I could never cease to be anything less than a proud Jew. Still, I feared that maybe there was a flaw to Judaism as I understood it, and that our ancestors died in vain defending against the untenable.

I continued to read my scriptures daily, and the power of God's Word restored my conviction that I would eventually find the answer. My faith grew and grew as it became increasingly obvious that the

Word was without error. Sooner or later I'd uncover the fallacy of Christianity. A loving, all-knowing, all-powerful and merciful God would not play such a dirty trick on humanity. The God of Israel was to be trusted, and if I remained faithful, He would show me where Christian dogma went astray.

Attending the Friday night studies conducted by Raymond Cohen in Clara's basement added a new dimension to my dilemma . . . not only were more questions raised about Jesus, but new thoughts bombarded me regarding those who claimed Him as Savior. I began to like and respect these "holy rollers" who, due to their reverence for God's Word, loved Israel and the Jewish people. Their feelings were far from superficial, and their genuine concern for my wellbeing was touching. How could I dislike those who prayed for me, not merely to win me over to their point of view, but that I might find the truth and peace? It wasn't easy to hold such sincere people in contempt.

Spending time with Clara and Joe brought more soul-searching. They were unabashedly Jewish in spite of their belief in Jesus. I never saw Clara without a Jewish star around her neck, and the small golden *mogen David* earrings in her lobes. She spoke to me in Yiddish, as well as English, and was always praising her *Yeshua*. Her mother, who was then in her eighties, was even smaller and rounder, and spoke a mixture of broken English mixed with Yiddish. With her marked European accent, and the same warmth and exuberance seen in Clara, she too praised her Jesus, the God of Israel.

I was growing more and more comfortable with the congregation that gathered on Friday evenings, and I no longer had a problem going downstairs when Clara led the singing. New songs were added from time to time, always written in phonetic Yiddish on large pieces of white cardboard. The tunes were catchy and glorifying to God, and even though *Yeshua* was the focus, I could deal with it a lot better. Perhaps they were all delusional, but wouldn't this be a better world if everyone had such love and conviction?

You may be able to sense how ambivalent I had become. One minute there was every possibility that this insanity made sense, and in the next breath, I was a *meshummed* (traitor) to have gotten so involved with these *meshuggenuh* (crazy) people. By this time my wife had made a profession of faith, and between her, her sister and my brother-in-law, I was the lone outsider and dissident. They made no bones about praying for my salvation, and I was grateful one minute and resentful the next.

Life could have been so sweet. We had a brand-new baby boy, and a brand-new home not far from my sister and brother in-law, and new friends. Ray's interests extended beyond the Bible, and we could spend hours and hours talking about many different topics. Things were going well on the job also, so why did Jesus have to be the fly in the ointment?

Some of my old friends and co-workers began to get annoyed with me, as I found it difficult not to talk about Jesus and the Bible. They thought this was obsessive, and that I was becoming a bore. My mother and twin sister were also expressing concern about my "sanctimonious" attitude and penchant for introducing the Bible into every conversation. Frankly, I loved my family dearly, but I was becoming far more comfortable with the new friends who shared my enthusiasm for God's word.

The inner conflict began to intrude upon my sleep. At night I was restless. Tossing and turning, I couldn't shut down my brain. Bible verses and prophetic passages about the messianic kingdom flashed in my head. If I dozed off, it was only to awake in a sweat, fearful that God was upset with me. If I were wrong in entertaining thoughts of Jesus' Lordship, I was about to be struck dead by a vengeful God who judged me to be unfaithful and unworthy. Yet, if Jesus were Lord, I would roast in hell for denying the Savior who shed His blood to reconcile me to a holy God. Being between a proverbial rock and a hard place is discomforting when you are trying to get much-needed sleep.

Subconsciously I knew that I had intellectually accepted the fact that Jesus is the One of Whom Moses and the prophets wrote. There could be no denying the plethora of scripture verses pointing to this truth. The problem was that it didn't matter. My Judaism was more precious to me than being right, and I could not betray my heritage. The unrest was relentless because I was not able to reconcile my profound feelings with the truth.

I literally began to think that I was going out of my mind. The words spoken by the prophet Elijah to the children of Israel gathered on Mount Carmel resonated in my head: "How long halt ye between two opinions? If the Lord be God, follow Him . . ." My sanity demanded that I make a decision. Falling to my knees, I confessed my fears and uncertainties to God, and promised that if Jesus were truly the Savior, I would follow Him regardless of how uncomfortable this made me. For the first time in my life I realized that truth was more important than anything else. I could never be at rest ignoring what I knew in my heart to be true. It was only when I finally subordinated my personal desire to what I knew was God's will that I had a restful sleep.

7

The Trial Of My Faith

Everybody rejoiced with me upon learning of my decision. They saw this as an answer to prayer, and knew of my relief after struggling so long with the conflict that raged within me. It was terrific to see such enthusiasm, and encouraging that so many could share my joy. Strangely, whereas all my friends and extended family were emotional, that was not the case with me. A sense of peace enveloped me, and I knew in my heart that I made the right decision. Still, there was no feeling of euphoria that I had seen with others coming to salvation. In a rather matter-of-fact way I knew what was true, so my experience was intellectual, rather than emotional. Nonetheless, I was rejoicing in my spirit.

A few days later Ray approached me with what I thought to be the icing on the cake. "How would you like to come to work for me in Connecticut?" he asked. What was there to think about? What would the Lord want more for me? Now that I was saved, I would be closer to my mentor and teacher, and have the opportunity to grow even more. There was no doubt in my mind that this was of the Lord, and I immediately responded in the affirmative. Judy and Lee had become so close that I was sure that Judy, too, would share my enthusiasm for such a move.

My wife never was one who liked change of any kind, and ordinarily contemplating a move like this would have been overwhelming. In addition, Judy loved our new home and would not have dreamed of leaving under any other circumstances. This was the one time in our lives that she was glad to consider uprooting and going to a different state. Certainly, there was to be no obstacle.

The air was let out of my balloon rather quickly by Ray's response to my immediate decision to move. He reminded me that nothing should ever be done without prayer. "Is this what the Lord would have you do?" he asked. What kind of question was this? Why wasn't it as obvious to Ray as it was to me? I resented the fact that he had to admonish me, but knew that he was much more tuned into spiritual matters. Reluctantly, and with some embarrassment, I agreed that I should seek the Lord before making a decision.

I did pray as promised, but never waited for God's response. Still confident that this was His plan for me, I set about to follow my predisposed intent. When I saw Ray the following Friday evening, I told him that I put my house on the market, and that if it sold within a reasonable time that I established, it would be evidence that God concurred. What I didn't tell Ray was that I set an asking price far below the true value of my home, so that I could help Jesus make a quick sale. As far as Ray knew, I put out a "fleece" and was willing to wait upon the Lord.

The designated time came and went without as much as a bite on the house. Not one phone call; not a solitary inquiry. I was puzzled and upset, and even Ray was not able to come up with a possible reason. Why did the Lord slam the door shut on what would have been an opportunity for me to benefit from a Godly relationship? Obviously distressed and upset by my lack of understanding, I dealt with the disappointment by reminding myself that Jesus didn't make mistakes. I only wished that He had given me a call to let me in on the secret!

Two weeks later Ray announced that he knew why this plan was not meant to be. "Marty," he said, "the Lord is sending me to Florida. If you had accepted this position, you would have sold your home and moved away from your family and friends, and be all alone in Connecticut. God has spared you from making such a mistake. Frankly, up to now I had no thought of relocating to Florida, but the Lord has shown me that He wants me to go into full-time ministry there. I'm leaving my job."

Talk about good news, bad news! Now I had my answer, but this was even worse. It was bad enough that I was not going to be working and living near my dearest friend, but how would I get by with him leaving New York? Judy was equally upset, since she and Lee had been inseparable. I couldn't understand why God didn't want me to work with Ray in Connecticut, and I certainly was astounded by the announcement that he was headed to Florida.

With all of this taking place, Ray approached me the following Friday evening to let me know that he believed that the Lord wanted me to take over the Friday classes after he left. That's all I needed. My mentor is leaving, the finest Bible teacher will no longer be providing the instruction and insight that was so instrumental to my growth, and now the responsibility would fall on my shoulders. No way! I assured Ray that in a million years I'd never become a teacher, preacher or public speaker, nor would I be able to handle such responsibility. Once more I was admonished by Ray: "Didn't you learn yet that you are to do nothing until you pray about it?"

Of course I knew the importance of prayer, and I was ashamed of myself. However, I was not about to subject myself to becoming a teacher. I reasoned that I was newly saved and had so much to learn that it would be presumptuous for me to teach others. The truth of the matter is that I never was able to stand in front of an audience and speak. Every time there were oral reports or school plays requiring performing in public, I would avoid showing up. Having all eyes focused on me made me so nervous that I would break out in a sweat, get stomach cramps and go blank. There was no way that I would make a fool of myself, and there was nothing to pray about.

While I did pray, in reality it was a forum to explain to God how unfair it was to expect me to become involved with something that made me sick and uncomfortable. He would have to understand that I was not rebellious or intransigent, but that His expectations (and Ray's) were unreasonable. It seemed to me that God was there to meet my needs, and not to intrude upon my life. Why then was I so upset, and why couldn't I put this behind me? I was not experiencing the peace of God, but I didn't want to believe that it was the consequence of my refusing to submit.

Clara came to me and asked that I reconsider, for it was her desire that someone with a strong Jewish background and *Yiddishkeit* continue the Friday classes. As much as I adored Clara and hated disappointing her, there was no way that I would change my mind. Since Ray was now gone, Clara contacted the ABMJ (American Board of Missions to the Jews), to arrange for a new Friday night teacher. The only one available was a Jewish man, Jonas Cohen (no relation to Raymond), who was well qualified. The problem with this was that Jonas spent a lot of his time on speaking engagements around the country, so he knew committing to a weekly class would be difficult.

Jonas taught the next Friday evening and approached me after the class to explain his concern about his busy schedule conflicting with this weekly Bible study. He fully understood and appreciated my fears, but asked that I reconsider. When I assured him that I had no change of heart, he simply asked me to pray that God would show me the right thing to do. Jonas merely wanted me to fill in for him when he couldn't be there, so I shouldn't be overwhelmed with the thought that I would be locked into a permanent situation.

This time I did pray, but I remained convinced that since I appeased God, He would not push me into an awkward and difficult situation. I was really shocked, therefore, to get a call that week telling me that Jonas was not going to be able to make it on Friday. I panicked and told Clara to get in touch with the ABMJ to send someone else. Try as they might, no one else was available, and toward the end of the week Clara let me know that unless I agreed to take over, there would be no Friday class that week.

I was in a turmoil; which was worse, to live with the guilt or to actually get up in front of a class? They were my friends and undemanding, but that did not offer much comfort. I avoided public speaking all my life, and nothing was going to make this palatable. Once again I told Clara that I couldn't do it, but I felt miserable. It was a toss-up as to which would be worse, to remain in this wretched state, or to serve God and make a fool of myself. I finally chose the latter, and with fear and trepidation planned a study for that Friday.

Don't ask me how I got through it, and don't expect me to tell you what I spoke about that night. In my mind I was frozen in time and felt like a jackass standing there with nothing coming out of my mouth. My mind seemed to go blank and my palms were ice cold. I was dripping wet and the sweat poured down my back. By the time I finished my shirt was soaked through and through. With all of this, I was assured by all that the study was interesting and informative. They said that I was a natural, and that my nervousness did not show.

I silently thanked God for getting me through this experience and relaxed, thinking that now I would be left alone. I did the right thing, so there would be no need for further testing. Little did I know that I would never see Jonas Cohen again, and that the temporary assignment filling in that Friday would last over twenty years. It is surprising to most who know me that no matter how many years I've been teaching, it is still an effort to get up in front of a crowd. I still sweat, get cramps and my hands become clammy and cold. Once I get started it gets a little better, but I'm always afraid of losing my train of thought and appearing stupid. While I enjoy teaching, and realize that it has been so instrumental to my personal growth, the side effects remain. It is compounded when I must address audiences with whom I am not familiar, but somehow the Lord sees me through it all. I am learning that His strength is made perfect in my weakness.

Teaching on a regular basis has been a blessing in disguise. It keeps me studying the word to prepare lessons and it forces me to be in constant prayer. After the lessons we sat around Clara's kitchen table, and had provocative discussions. When new people were brought to the class, it was my job to answer their questions and to support the Jewishness of scripture and Jesus. All that I had been through in struggling with the christological implications of Jesus' ministry was now being put to good use. I enjoyed this part of the evening best of all.

Once again I thought life was good, and that I somehow passed the test. My faith was tried, and I survived. I never suspected that the trials were far from over. In fact, it wasn't long before my perfect little world started to crumble. All my problems were traceable to my belief in Jesus. While I remained firm in my conviction, I couldn't fathom why Jesus would allow me to have so many problems. Getting saved was supposed to be the end of one's problems, not the start.

At the Friday classes, and on my job, I was often sharing Bible truths with those who knew very little. They marveled at my knowledge of scripture, and it was a blessing to see those who came to faith. The time was ripe to speak to my family about Jesus. No doubt they would be impressed with how much I had learned. Realizing how difficult it was for me when I first started, I expected similar resistance, but I was not prepared for the reaction that followed. My mother and sister were shocked to say the least, and could not comprehend how I had been brainwashed. *"Chuchom"* ("Smart one"), my mother exclaimed, "already you know more than the rabbis."

My mother and sister became exasperated by my attempt to press the issue, and finally demanded that the subject be dropped. For the longest time afterwards, this was a sword hanging over my head, and the loving relationship was severely strained. In the back of our minds our relationship had changed, but we could not discuss the reasons openly. The only time Christianity or Jesus was broached by my family was to make a sarcastic remark of how I had changed so drastically. I made it a practice to attend synagogue on the High Holy Days with my mother and sister, just as I had always done, but they still perceived me to be a *goy* (gentile). It took years for them to realize that I never stopped being Jewish, and did not cease from being a strong supporter of Israel. This helped normalize relations, but an invisible barrier remained.

When things quieted down with my family, I told my wife, Judy, that it was time to speak to her mother and father. My brother and sister-in-law had never dared to bring up this subject. My in-laws suspected something, but avoided a confrontation. They had mentioned to us that Myra and Ron were never home on Sunday mornings, speculating that they went to church. Since Ron was Italian and a Catholic, they were not all that surprised. They also realized that Myra had always been rebellious, so they overlooked the suspicions and avoided controversy.

Judy knew that I was opening up a hornet's nest, since she had borne the burden of her mother's tirades against the intermarriage of her sister. Whereas the passing years brought acceptance for a good-natured and sensitive son-in-law, the fact of his being a non-Jew would always be a bone of contention. God forbid a million times that the children would not be raised Jewish. Thus Judy was most reluctant to agree finally that we should speak to her folks about what had taken place in our lives.

We took the opportunity to invite not only our in-laws to discuss something of "great importance", but to ask another couple who were our dearest friends. We all sat down in the den of our home, and I started to tell them how we had been studying the Bible and had come to realize that Jesus is the Messiah of whom Moses and the prophets had spoken. Before too much else could be said, the shouting and ranting began. My mother-in-law was outraged, and she turned to my father-in-law in a fit of anger. "Jack, get our coats," she demanded, "we're leaving."

Judy ran after her mother and grabbed her arm as she was opening the door. Her mother spun around and gave my wife a hard slap across the face, slamming the door behind her. We were all in shock. In spite of realizing her mother's volatility, we certainly did not expect such a display. Judy was always the good daughter who was gentle and compliant; the exemplary child who never caused one second of grief to her doting mother. But now she had put a knife through her mother's heart.

The other couple, who were Jewish, were equally dismayed. They excused themselves and left shortly thereafter, making it clear that there was to be no further discussion on this topic. We had expected them to be much more open, as their daughter was seeing a gentile boy. How could we have misjudged so badly? And, I was to blame. My wife reminded me that this was all my idea, and she never should have listened.

In the years that followed, my mother-in-law decided that every problem that ever arose in the family was my fault. In fact, I was responsible for poisoning the minds of both her daughters, as well as her son-in-law who would have been content to embrace Judaism, if it were not for me. Ironically, years ago my mother-in-law's younger sister had married a Catholic who converted to Judaism. My mother-in-law sent her sister's converted husband to visit my brother-in-law to convince him to convert as well. You can well imagine her dismay with me, who, having been born a Jew, was now a gentile in her eyes.

What else could go wrong? I didn't know when to leave well enough alone, and now relationships were severely strained with both our families. Whereas we did make our peace with Judy's mom and dad, my mother-in-law incessantly made remarks about my being a *meshummed* (traitor) and that I was no longer a Jew. When I attempted to defend myself, she shouted, "I don't want to hear it!" It's sad that not much changed over the years, insofar as this reaction is concerned.

Years later my in-laws retired to Florida, and we all chipped in to help them financially. This changed nothing regarding my mother-in-law's contempt for my belief. This ill will even extended to her sister's attitude towards me. When my father-in-law passed away, his body was flown to New York to be buried. The *shiva* (mourning period) was observed at my sister-in-law's home on the North Shore of Suffolk County. My mother-in-law's sister had come to pay her respects, but was to spend the evening with her brother who resided about forty minutes away in Nassau County. Since I lived in Queens, and had to pass that way, I offered to take her. However, she insisted that my brother-in-law make the trip there and back, rather than go with me. She would sooner inconvenience my brother-in-law than accept a ride from an apostate Jew.

I guess that this still was not enough to build character, so Jesus allowed some more adverse circumstances to be added to the equation. We started running into all kinds of car problems. Since we lived on Long Island and I worked in New York City, we needed two cars. One or the other was constantly breaking down, and the cost of repairs was keeping us in debt. We purchased a number of used vehicles, but within a short time, something went wrong with each of them. Our high mortgage, the cost of commutation and the maintenance of the cars combined to create a financial nightmare. Things like this were not supposed to happen to believers. All of life's problems dissolve when you trust God, so what was going on?

Having no success with old, used cars, we decided to purchase a new one. This meant taking out a three-year car loan. It might be an additional expense, but it had to be better than being nickeled and dimed to death repairing the used cars. I picked up a leftover Volkswagen that was one year old, with the new models being introduced. God would bless such a responsible selection, after all the savings in gas would help offset the monthly payment.

The following Friday evening my wife and I were driving to Clara's home in my new little VW. As I was making the turn from the main road to the cross street near Clara, a car ran the red light and hit us broadside. Our little "bug" was totaled. I hit my head on the windshield which shattered, sending my glasses flying into the night. Judy's side of the car was so badly smashed that she had to be cut out with an acetylene torch. She was not able to move her feet, and they put her on a gurney to bring her to the hospital. I was in a daze from the impact, and couldn't see much without my glasses.

My concern was for Judy, as she had blood running down her legs, and could not feel them. However, shortly after being treated at the emergency room, she was on her feet and walking. Only some minor cuts and bruises attested to the accident. I was so relieved, and I praised God for her being OK. The attention then turned to me, as the doctor wanted to examine me. I assured him that I was all right, but he insisted that he check me over. Upon removing my jacket, we all observed that I had blood on my shirt. This surprised me, since I felt only stiffness and a little bruising. At the doctor's command I then took my shirt off, and he wiped away the blood from my chest and shoulder.

The doctor looked very puzzled for there wasn't a mark on my body! "How can that be?" he asked in disbelief. "There was no blood on your jacket, and no cut on your body, but look at this blood on your shirt." I knew what had happened, and I told him that Jesus healed me. I then spent about twenty minutes telling him about my being a Jewish believer in Jesus, the God of Israel. He listened attentively, and I was surprised that he did not scoff at what I said.

The following week, when I was sharing this with Clara, she told me that one of the members of the class had seen the accident, and told the others. They all spent the evening holding us up in prayer. She also asked me the name of the doctor who treated me. When I told her, she smiled broadly and revealed that she knew him, and that she had shared the gospel with him on more than one occasion. In spite of all the trauma, God had wrought good from this experience.

If this were not enough, let me explain further how God blessed this seemingly horrible event. After all, I should have mentioned that the person who owned the car that struck us did not have insurance. To make matters worse, I had just picked up the VW, and the insurance was not placed yet. Now I had three years of car payments, but no car! *"Oy veiz meir* (Woe is me)! What else can go wrong?" My finances were a shambles to begin with; now how was I to survive?

I'll get back to that in a moment, but first let's look at what's really exciting. I had been terribly addicted to smoking. It was not just a disgusting habit that controlled me, but I was concerned that it interfered with my relationship with God. I had been praying that the Lord would help me, and yet I knew that it was a choice that I would have to make. Thus, I prayed that if Jesus would take the first step and get me started, I would make a concerted effort to quit for good. For those of you have gone through similar circumstances, I'm sure you know how hard it is. I had been smoking since the age of twelve, and by this time was consuming three and a half packs of cigarettes daily.

So here I was, back home following the accident, and I reached for a cigarette, but found none. Not only had I lost my glasses, but my cigarettes as well. I had no car to drive to the store to pick some up, and it would mean walking at least four or five miles to find a place open that sold cigarettes. Under normal circumstances that would not have stopped me. The urge to smoke was greater than any inconvenience, and it was not unusual for me to go out in the middle of the night to satisfy my longing to smoke. This time, however, I knew that my prayer had been answered, not exactly as I had envisioned, but in such a manner as to make it clear that God was involved. The initial step had been taken, and now I would go on to conquer an addiction.

God's grace went even beyond that. One might say that without supporting such an expensive habit, I would have more money to pay my bills. On the other hand, I still was minus a car, and had payments to make. I also had a lot of other bills that were backing up, and I was never in worse financial shape in my life. Surely it couldn't get worse. Some of you may remember the quip, "Cheer up, things could be worse. So I cheered up, and sure enough, they got worse." How apropos; it <u>did</u> get worse. The Lord took this opportunity to let me know that I must trust Him implicitly, and that included tithing my income, which I had never done.

For several months I had been struggling with the concept of tithing, but I put it on the back burner due to my financial circumstances. There was no doubt that I would have to come to terms with this, as well as anything else the Lord put on my plate, but I reasoned that this was not a high priority. Now, with all that had taken place, I knew I had to respond. It just seemed so unfair that the timing was so incredibly poor.

Please do not think that I am trying to impress you with how holy I can be. If anything, I'm a coward. When I see the hand of God in a situation, I'm afraid not to listen. Since, as they say, discretion is the better part of valor, I decided to comply and, at that point in life, I began to tithe. In fact, I challenged God and told Him that since this was so absurd, He now had the responsibility to take care of me. I would never be able to make it on my own.

There was a couple who came faithfully to the Friday night classes. Their name was Jacobs, and though it may sound Jewish, they were not. The Jacobs loved the Lord, and loved the Jewish people. We enjoyed a warm relationship with them, and without our knowledge, they took up a love offering to help us purchase a replacement vehicle. The following Friday they handed me a white envelope with money inside. Charlie Jacobs added that he had a dear friend who owned a used car lot, and that he had spoken to him on my behalf. The following day Charlie brought me there to look at the cars on the lot.

I had never bothered to check the contents of the envelope, and had no idea how much was inside. I also had no idea how I would pay the difference between the cost of any car I selected and the amount in the envelope. It was simply at Charlie's insistence that I accompanied him to this used car dealer. And it was Charlie who influenced me to select the car we chose. By now you might even have guessed that the cost of this automobile was three hundred dollars, the exact amount inside the envelope. Right then I knew in my heart that when it comes to tithing, you can never out-give Jesus.

8

More Pain, More Gain

When I was a child I did things to please my parents out of a pure motive. I loved them dearly and derived pleasure from making them happy. They *kvelled* (demonstrated great pride) when I did something considerate without having to be asked. It might have been doing the dishes or going out early in the morning to wash my father's car. The look on their faces was my reward.

I wish that I could say that my motives in serving God were as pure. The sad truth is that more often than not, I acted out of a sense of responsibility or a fear of displeasing Him. My concept of right and wrong served as the impetus, not a free-loving spirit. It took a long time to translate the desire to please my earthly father into seeking to bring that kind of joy to my heavenly Father. How sad that I didn't give Him a reason to *kvell*.

I was doing the right things in that I was teaching on a regular basis, reading and studying the Word, and being an active witness to all who would listen. Now that I was tithing, my finances were getting squared away, and I might add that since I took this step, I have not had financial stress as in the past. If anything, God has blessed me beyond my wildest imagination. Not that I'm rich, but my wife and I have enjoyed a good middle-class life that would seem to be luxurious in comparison to my childhood years. I even felt good about myself in having conquered a smoking addiction that plagued me for so long. This was not only important to my relationship with the Lord, but I wanted to set a good example for my son.

Ray and Lee Cohen had relocated to south Florida, and to my surprise, I didn't fall apart. Whereas I was overwhelmed at the outset, I learned that my trust is in the Lord and not in man. Sure, there was a sense of loss, since they were such dear friends and had been so instrumental to our growth, but life went on. I thank God that I still had Clara to keep me on my spiritual toes. When I had time, I would drive out to Huntington Station just to have a cup of coffee with her and to talk about the things of God. Clara's stories about her many years in ministry were exciting and inspirational. Please remember that a Jew who believed in Jesus was practically unheard-of back then.

During my visits to Clara, usually accompanied by my young son, Clara would ask me to drive her into town where the stores were. As we walked along, she would stop when we came to a business owned by Jewish people. Taking my son's hand, she would declare that she'd watch him for me. Then she would shove me through the door and tell me to go tell the owner about Jesus. Clara was so intimidating and forceful that you did as you were told, regardless of how embarrassing it might be.

Since all seemed to be well, it was time for my next test. Ray indicated that Judy and I should give serious thought to being baptized. Clara picked up on this and said she would arrange for us to be baptized at the mission of the ABMJ (American Board of Missions to the Jews). "Not so fast," I said, "we'll need some time to pray about it." Actually, that was a pious dodge that in reality meant I needed to give this some thought. What were the implications to a little Jewish boy from the Bronx going through the waters of baptism?

As much as Ray reminded me that baptism was traceable to the Jewish custom of the *mikveh* (ritual bathing and purification), it was of little comfort. In the mind of the Jew, baptism is the ultimate act of separating oneself from Judaism. It is the personification of conversion and the denial of the faith of one's ancestors. Thousands of Jews died *al kiddush ha-Shem* (for the sanctity of God's name) rather than suffer baptism, and I was expected to ignore such powerful emotions. Over the centuries baptism was forced upon our people if they wished to live; it certainly would be unconscionable to undergo this rite on a voluntary basis.

Judy and I did discuss and pray over the matter, and once again I agreed because it was clear from God's Word that such action is appropriate. This was to be seen as nothing more than an open testimony to my identifying with the death, burial and resurrection of Jesus. Under those circumstances, I could not say no, but I was not enthralled with the concept. When the day came, we took the trip to the Manhattan headquarters of the ABMJ. There were several others scheduled for immersion that day, and although they were somewhat apprehensive, they looked forward with joy to entering into a more meaningful relationship with their Savior. I felt no such joy, but was resigned to doing what was right. Each of the others gave stirring testimonies as to what this meant to them, and they were radiant upon emerging from the water. Neither my wife nor I were enthusiastic or responsive; we went through the motions and were glad when it was over. I just prayed silently that my family would never find out what we had done.

Since that time I have been asked to speak at several baptisms, both at the ABMJ and those conducted through the ministry of *Beth Yeshua* (House of Jesus). Preparing meaningful messages for the occasion has given me new insights and understanding of the importance of what I had undergone, and remorse for having approached such a sacred ritual with mere resolution. More importantly, I think back to my mechanical approach to the chance to identify with my Lord and Savior, and feel badly that Jesus received no *nachas* (joy or pleasure) from His child.

Shortly after this event, I was invited back to the mission by Clara to speak at another baptism. A number of people from the same family were all undergoing baptism together. Clara had taken this group under her wing, and she was discipling these new believers whom she helped bring to faith. All were former Catholics, and they lived in the eastern part of Suffolk County. Dutifully, I agreed, but as usual I didn't have much enthusiasm for the task. I felt that my calling was to the Jew, and I had no burden for unsaved gentiles. There were thousands of missions all over the world for the gentiles, but very few for the Jews. It never occurred to me that all the lost go to hell, regardless of ethnicity. That awakening was to come later.

I met the Saxon clan on the appointed Sunday, when Clara introduced me in the anteroom where the candidates were preparing for baptism. At Clara's insistence, we hugged and kissed; something I found embarrassing since I didn't know these people. However, Clara's usual enthusiasm and jocular manner smoothed things over, and the day went well. Both my wife and I enjoyed the time of fellowship with those who were perfect strangers at the outset.

The following Friday, and for many to come, the members of the Saxon family showed up for our Bible study. Identical twin brothers, Richard and Robert, along with their wives, both named Patty, became regulars. More often than not, they *shlepped* along their sisters and brothers-in-law, as well as other friends and neighbors. The Saxons had an insatiable appetite for the Word, and we spent hours upon hours after the study talking about the scriptures. Even though they were Catholics, they wanted to learn more about their Jewish roots. No doubt this interest had been stimulated by Clara's teaching.

Clara and a member of the ABMJ teaching staff went out weekly to conduct a mid-week Bible study at Richie's home in Holtsville. The group couldn't get enough of the teaching, and a number still attended the Friday class as well. There are some from the original group who still join in a Bible study that I conduct in Suffolk County to this day.

Things were running smoothly, so it was time for more testing. Clara approached me to fill in one week for the regular teacher who led the study in Holtsville. This was quite a trip for me, and it meant doubling the time spent that week in preparing studies and speaking. I was not exactly enthusiastic about such a project. Remember, I was more interested in reaching Jews, so this was not, as far as I could see, consistent with my ministry. Nonetheless, I somewhat reluctantly agreed, comforted by the thought that it was for only one week. My attitude, as usual, gave the Lord nothing to *kvell* about.

The study went well, and was received with enthusiasm. Since I was always apprehensive about speaking, particularly when I didn't know the people well, it was a relief. I was glad that it was over and said goodnight to all. As I was leaving, Richie said, "See you next week." I stopped in my tracks, not believing what I was hearing. What was he talking about? I agreed to fill in for one week. Did he know something that I didn't? Sure enough, I learned from Clara that this "gig" was being extended "slightly", and I was stuck. It would have been too embarrassing to tell the exuberant group that I had no intention of returning.

As was the case with the Huntington Station class that was to be temporary, I became the permanent temp. That mid-week study lasted for years and years, but not necessarily on the same evening. We made a number of adjustments over the course of time, but teaching twice a week became the routine. When Clara ultimately moved to Florida, this became my Friday evening class. I had grown to love them so much that I endured a trip that took on the average two-and-a-half hours in stop-and-go traffic. Fortunately, the return trip took only an hour-and-a-half, since the traffic abated in the later evening. There were times when it took as much as four hours due to the summer traffic to the Hamptons.

The Saxon boys and their wives continued to reach out to relatives, friends, neighbors and co-workers. Our class grew and grew, and Richie's large basement could not accommodate all. The younger children had to sit on pillows strewn on the floor, but nobody complained. Both Clara and I rejoiced in the growth in numbers and the spiritual growth as well. It bothered me that such eager people with a thirst to know God were getting short-changed with nothing more than a weekly Bible study. It was clear that they longed for a lot more. Clara continued to work with the women, emphasizing sanctification, but this too had its limitations.

Little did I know that God was already making preparations without letting me in on the secret. In order to see His hand in this, permit me to go off on a slight tangent for a moment. Ray and Lee Cohen had settled into an ABMJ-sponsored ministry in south Florida, but it wasn't long before some complications evolved. To their dismay, conflicts arose, which made them miserable. Without spending unproductive time on the details, suffice it to say that it led to a parting of the ways. Ray and Lee were devastated; after all, they had left a comfortable lifestyle in Norwalk, Connecticut to relocate. Ray had an excellent executive position with a successful corporation, and he gave that up for a fraction of the money he was to receive in serving the Lord. Why would God do this to him?

Joe, Clara, Ray, Lee and I were vigilant in prayer, and waited for the leading of the Lord. Ray then informed me that God put it upon his heart to start a new outreach. This became the American Messianic Mission, Inc., also known as *Beth Yeshua* (House of Jesus, or House of Salvation). He had been teaching Bible studies at an outreach called "His Place", to mostly young, often-dysfunctional boys and girls who were on drugs and/or alcohol. These troubled teens became the nucleus of the new ministry. Throw in for good measure some adults attending "Neurotics Anonymous" and you have the remainder of the cast of characters.

Although there were not many Jews, Raymond was determined to teach from that frame of reference. He had always taught me that if you present the Bible from its Jewish perspective, both Jew and gentile will benefit. On the contrary, it is the gentile alone who benefits when the spiritual and historical Jewish context is ignored. To help make it comfortable for unsaved Jews (and others as well), the large room was set up like a living room with chairs and sofas. Beth Yeshua would be an informal and comfortable setting for the uninitiated to attend. God blessed and prospered the ministry, and I rejoiced greatly as Ray and Lee kept us updated as to what was taking place.

Shortly after this Ray and Lee invited me to come down to Florida to be the guest speaker at the dedication of their new facility. They didn't have to ask twice. I hadn't seen them in a while, and was eager to spend some quality time with them. The thought of going to sunny Florida didn't hurt, either. Since the Cohens had a spare bedroom in their condo, it cost me nothing to have this mini-vacation and spiritual shot-in-the-arm. We talked into the wee hours of the morning each day that I was there.

The young adults that I met were nothing as I had imagined, considering the backgrounds from whence they came. Studying scripture and sound counsel from the Cohens brought spiritual growth and inspired responsibility. Now that they could get high on Jesus, drugs and alcohol were forsaken. These were young men and women learning to take their place in society. They were also enthusiastic and faithful witnesses on the streets of Fort Lauderdale, and wherever else they went. Mothers and fathers of problem children testified, with tearful eyes, of the transformation that was taking place in their children.

I felt very close to this group, as well as with the older folks who attended. The common bond of the love of Jesus was a cord that bound us all together with a sense that something remarkable was taking place. It was not easy to say goodbye and to return to New York. I wanted so much to be part of what I considered to be a glorious work that lifted up the name of Jesus. At that point, however, I could only offer financial support and prayer.

Not long afterward, I was given another excuse to return to Florida. Ray had decided to hold a retreat for his congregants. It was to be held over a three-day period at a retreat center a few hours north of Fort Lauderdale. This meant flying down to Fort Lauderdale the night before and spending the night with the Cohens. We would leave the next morning by car for the facility, and remain until Sunday afternoon so that I could catch a flight back to New York to be at work on Monday. It was exciting that I would be able to spend time with my dear friends, and the only drawback was that I was to be the main speaker, leaving me with a lot of messages to prepare. Having that much responsibility was frightening, but I wanted very much to be part of this retreat.

I had never been on a retreat and had no idea of what to expect. It proved to be a major crossroad in my life, and I have never been the same since. For the first time I realized that being saved was only the beginning of a journey that was meant to be one of continuous growth. When Jesus said that we were to seek first the kingdom of God and His righteousness, He really meant just that. My eyes opened up to a renewed sense of purpose and a burning desire to make a difference with my life. Most of all, I wanted my heavenly Father to have some *nachas* (pleasure) from me.

Those three days I got to know people like never before. We not only attended meetings three times a day; we ate together, we slept together, we prayed together and enjoyed other activities together. In the evenings we had giant bonfires, toasted marshmallows, and roasted franks and hamburgers. Late into the night we talked, praised the Lord and sang hymns to our wonderful Messiah. But all of this, as grand as it was, was nothing in comparison to what took place at our meetings.

With the sharing of the Word came confessions of sin and requests for forgiveness. Many who formerly harbored dislike and resentment towards fellow believers were constrained to make things right with the Lord and with those who were the objects of the latent hostility. There were tears of joy that come from the sense of release, and hugging and kissing as relationships were mended and solidified. What was initially a congregation of strangers who lived fifteen hundred miles away became family. Every subsequent retreat and trip to Florida was perceived by me as coming home. Long after Ray was taken home to be with the Lord, and I succeeded him as president of the AMMI (the American Messianic Mission, Inc.), I continued to make at least four or five trips a year to visit my Florida family and to share God's Word with them.

I didn't know it at the time, but as I mentioned, the retreat changed my life and impacted what was to take place upon my return to New York. The Holtsville group immediately realized something dramatic happened which left an indelible impression. This was the start of what my life was to be dedicated to thereafter.

As a postscript to this chapter dealing with trials and growth, there are two thoughts that are worthy of mention. First, there were many other severe trials that I experienced, but for very personal reasons I don't feel at liberty to detail. Other people are involved and it would not be proper to go into circumstances that would divulge information best kept private. Suffice it to say, the things to which I allude were nothing short of monumental, and I want the reader to know that the Lord stood by me in every instance. Through every seemingly unbearable circumstance Jesus was there for me, and I can only join the chorus of all who sing with conviction "How Great Thou Art".

I would be remiss not to mention that it never ceases to amaze me how God put up with such an insufferable and arrogant individual as I. For years I listened to testimonies of those who, often in tears, would proclaim God's mercy in bringing them out from drug addiction, alcoholism, adultery, abusive behavior and other perversions. Surely, I thought, they had much for which to be grateful. By comparison, God was fortunate indeed to have someone like me. After all, I was not a wife-beater or child molester; I never was even tempted to try marijuana, and I doubt that I had as much as two beers in my entire life. Perhaps I was a sinner by definition, but cleaning me up was nothing in comparison to the job the Lord had cut out for Himself with those others!

I find it difficult to believe how long it took me to realize the scope of God's mercy and forgiveness in my life. In spite of intensive study, years of teaching and preaching and witnessing, I had no clue as to the heinous nature of my sin. I was well aware that I had been guilty of cursing the name of Jesus, and having hate and contempt for Him and Christianity, yet this too was justifiable or mitigated by the anti-Semitism to which I had been subjected. Should you look up the word "jerk" in the dictionary, don't be surprised if you see my picture. And, if anybody reading this happens to know me personally, and believe that I'm not all that different now than I was before, please be patient, because God isn't through with me yet.

9

Beth Yeshua Travels North

The next time I met with my Holtsville family I spoke with passion and zeal regarding what had taken place in Florida. It was so infectious that they joined in the excitement. Without forethought, it suddenly occurred to me that the Saxons and company needed a Beth Yeshua to step up to the next level of growth. I encouraged them to have Raymond Cohen come up north to discuss this as a possibility. Needless to say, all concurred and the rest is history.

It was clear to us that the opportunity to grow spiritually was of paramount importance, and that Ray had the gift of organizing, teaching and laying the right foundation. Based upon a commitment from the regulars in attendance, we proceeded to rent a place in Patchogue, Long Island, where the studies and worship were to take place. Ray would spend several months in New York getting things started, and would later send an elder from his Florida congregation to take over. My role was to continue to teach at least once a week and to see that Beth Yeshua maintained its direction toward Jewish outreach. We were both a congregation of Jews and gentiles who were one in the Lord, and an evangelical outreach to the lost sheep of the house of Israel.

God prospered this endeavor, and new faces kept coming all the time. Richie and his brother Bobby were now working for the Long Island Railroad, and they were bold in their witness on the job. Before long so many were getting saved through that unique ministry that we dubbed the LIRR "the soul train". A good number of those who found Jesus on the train started to attend the Patchogue facility, and it wasn't long before we needed larger quarters. In time both Richie and Bobby were ordained as elders. To this day Bobby, who now holds an executive position with the railroad, is still active and teaches scripture to fellow LIRR employees.

Richie had an amazing desire to learn more about the Jewishness of scripture, which extended to his personal study of Talmudical commentaries. He ultimately became the full-time pastor, and left his job on the railroad. Richie labored to put together an outline about the

Talmud, its Biblical significance and how the writings speak of Israel's Messiah. He has since relocated to Michigan, but we remain the best of friends, and he still calls upon me from time to time to garner material for his teaching. He never lost his heart for the Jew or his understanding that it is through the Jewish frame of reference that we best understand the teachings of Jesus.

Fortunately, we were not only seeing spiritual growth in the congregation, but as a result of teaching Jewish evangelism and preaching and teaching classes, we were raising up more teachers. Besides Richie and Bobby Saxon, their brother-in-law Ralph Curtin became an excellent teacher and was later ordained as well. Today he is a full-time pastor of a Baptist church in Pompano Beach, Florida, where he continues to teach the Jewishness of our Lord and Savior. I've had the pleasure of attending Ralph's church along with Clara on a number of occasions. I'm so pleased to see that that congregation recognizes and respects Clara as Ralph's *yiddisha* mama.

Another contingent of worshippers and teachers came from one of our members who worked for the Internal Revenue Service in Holtsville. In fact, the part-time pastor of the ministry now in Floral Park, New York, is also a full-time employee of the IRS, as is one of our deacons. There are others as well who took basic training at Beth Yeshua, went on to seminary and now are in full-time ministry. Considering the fact that we are relatively small, the number of those who have gone on to serve as pastors, deacons and missionaries is disproportionate.

Some of those who attended the ministry in Suffolk had relatives in Nassau County. This led to starting a home Bible study in Nassau, and, in turn, led to another outreach of Beth Yeshua in Mineola, New York. This eventually became Beth Yeshua of Floral Park, where we are now. It is interesting that even as I write this, we are not certain how long we can remain here. Our landlord has put the building up for sale and we remain in prayer to see where the Lord would have us go. With His help, we pray that we can go on, and that we can continue to bring about an awareness that the gospel must be presented to the Jews in a meaningful way.

In order to promote the importance of reaching the Jewish people with the gospel, I speak from the pulpits of those churches in the tri-state area that share Beth Yeshua's concern for the Jews. It continues to frustrate me that very few of the churches in such a large area exhibit much interest in this endeavor. Most argue that the gospel is the gospel and Jesus can save Jews without a special outreach. It makes me wonder why churches see the need to raise up and support missionaries to China, Greece, Russia, etc., but they deem Jewish outreach to have little or no merit. Learning the customs and cultures of other nations is important, but most churches stop short of making this application to the Jewish people. I'm convinced that this results from Satan's wiles and influence, coupled with ignorance of God's plan to use the Jews as *Or Lagoyim*, the light to the nations.

A former member of our Mineola congregation invited me to speak at her home Bible study a couple of years ago. This lovely lady and her husband have a beautiful home in King's Point, Long Island, and they offer a catered supper followed by a Bible study on Tuesday evenings. What started out to be a guest appearance to teach Jewish outreach has evolved into another regular study which usually results in teaching there once or twice a month. I sit back and wonder sometimes how reluctant I was to become a teacher, and laugh to see how much of my time is spent doing just that. In addition to my regular weekly and bi-monthly classes, I take the pulpit at Beth Yeshua from time to time, speak at area churches, conduct seminars and do occasional interviews on Christian talk radio like WFME and WMCA.

Perhaps the most important part of the Beth Yeshua outreach has been our annual Passover *seder*. This is usually the best-attended function of the year, which requires much preparation and prayer. It provides the most splendid opportunity to present Jesus from a prophetic perspective, and to show how He truly is the lamb of God slain from the foundation of the world. My previous book goes into great detail on this topic, so I will not be repetitive. Let me add, though, that I am not aware of any similar outreach. While other ministries conduct *seders*, I've yet to be informed of any that are as comprehensive as the BY *seder*. We read from the traditional Passover *Haggadah* (a book with the order of service) in both the Hebrew and English so that the unsaved Jews who are invited can see our faithfulness to tradition. During the course of the reading we share meaningful commentary that is germane to our beliefs. Afterwards we explain how everything that took place, including the elements of the *seder* plate, relate to Jesus.

Due to the success of our *seders*, we started conducting similar types of gatherings to celebrate the other two of the *shlosh reglaim* (three annual pilgrimage festivals spoken of in Leviticus): *Shavuos* (Pentecost, or the Feast of Weeks) and *Succos* (the Feast of Booths, or Tabernacles). Since the law is "the shadow of things to come", we take advantage of the holiday studies to help our Jewish brothers and sisters to see the unfolding of God's plan, while enriching the gentile believers with insights not usually brought to their attention. Our outreach includes similar teachings on most of the other Jewish holidays and festivals, but without the meals and singing.

The teaching of Beth Yeshua is supplemented by a monthly newsletter that we call the *AMMI*. This is not only the initials of the American Messianic Mission, Inc., but the word "*ammi*" in Hebrew is "My People". I try to write at least two articles for each edition which helps others understand the heart and mind of the Jew, how all relates to Jesus, and the necessity to grow in grace and knowledge. The articles contributed by the congregation are usually homey and light tidbits as to what is going on at BY. Since I continue to be employed on a full-time basis, all this activity tends to keep me out of trouble.

I would be less than forthright not to add that I have the most profound respect for other ministries that have been so effective in reaching Jewish people and in glorifying the name of Jesus. Beth Yeshua pales in comparison to those outreaches which have accomplished so much. First and foremost is the granddaddy of them all, the ABMJ, which dates back before the turn of the last century. Leopold Cohn and Joseph Hoffman Cohn were visionaries who, under the most stringent conditions, broke ground and paved the way for all that followed. So many of the outreaches that exist today were started by men who got their training at the ABMJ.

Perhaps the single most influential work that has surfaced, the one that put Jewish evangelism on the map, is Jews For Jesus. They have become a household name unlike any other, and much credit is to be given to Moshe Rosen and his staff who were so innovative and creative in their bold advertising and tract distribution ministries. When I was first saved, not a soul was aware of Jews who believed that Jesus is the Messiah. Today, whenever I witness to a stranger, the first question invariably is, "Are you a Jew For Jesus?" I am confident that many of you have had the same experience.

How can we not admire others who have come to national prominence, like Arnold Fruchtenbaum of Ariel Ministries and Ellwood McQuaid, the executive director of Israel My Glory? There are more whose names are recognizable, whereas Beth Yeshua by comparison is a well-kept secret. Every once in a while someone will nod knowingly when I mention my name or that of Beth Yeshua, but then they confess that they had me or the work confused with one of a similar name. I am not exactly thrilled to be the head of an outreach that has reduced in size, rather than one that has experienced growth. The work in Florida where it all started is no longer around, and the outreach in Suffolk has disappeared as well.

There have been many years of frustration when we gave thought to shutting the doors due to lack of funds and seeming lack of interest. Close friends advised me to throw in the towel, and I was convinced on more than one occasion that the end was near. We still put our faith in the Lord, and have never used the old standby that God's work would be shut down unless more financial support is forthcoming. We depend solely upon the tithes of the congregation and never make pleas for money in our literature or in our services. I never received direction from God that it was time to call it quits. To this day we press on, trusting that God alone will decide when we are through.

When I have a bad day, I somehow am reminded that all heaven rejoices when a single soul comes to salvation. It is then that I draw consolation from the fact that hundreds have been saved through the outreach of Beth Yeshua. We also draw consolation from the fact that teachers, preachers and missionaries were trained by our staff, and that God is being served. Every one of the saved souls is precious and special in the sight of God. Who knows if the next leader who is to have an impact in evangelization will not be someone inspired or encouraged by the efforts of BY?

10

I Gain And Lose A Brother

Approximately thirteen years had gone by, and none of our family had heard a word from my brother. We had no idea where he had gone, and to all intents and purposes, he had fallen off the face of the earth. He caused a lot of pain to us all; the wife and children he left behind, and a mother, sister and brother who, as a result of his cowardice, couldn't even see his children. My love for my older brother was still there, but I had lost respect for the manner in which he handled his problems. Nonetheless, I understood God's forgiveness in my own life and I could forgive my brother. Primarily, when my thoughts turned to him, I felt pity more than anything else.

It was a Sunday evening and my wife and I were enjoying a quiet time as the weekend was drawing to a close. The phone rang, and to my utter amazement, it was my brother, Bernie, who had not contacted me in all this time. I can't say with any certainty exactly what was going through my mind, but to say the least, I was in shock. There were a million questions that I wanted to ask, but inherently I knew that I had to be careful not to say something that would sound judgmental or frighten him away. My instincts were to do all within my power to remain calm, and encourage him to re-establish the caring relationship that had once been important to us both. Although I didn't know it at the time, he reached out to me first, before trying to reach my mom or my sister. The way I handled this would effect us all.

I asked one simple question: "Where are you?" He gave me the name of a hotel in Manhattan, and I simply stated that I would be there in about an hour. I can't remember what I did with my son, but I must have arranged for someone to watch him. I remember only that my heart was racing, and that I shouted to my wife to get dressed immediately. We were going to the city to see my brother.

As I sped to New York on the Long Island Expressway, my wife knew that it was not a time for talking. I drove quickly, and so many thoughts were racing through my head that it would have been impossible to carry on an intelligent conversation. Judy gave me my space, and I concentrated on getting there in one piece, and before my brother would have a change of heart.

We met Bernie and his new wife in the lobby of the hotel. I threw my arms around his neck and we hugged and kissed. Through the tears and sighs of relief, we assured each other how good it was to get together. When we caught our breath, Bernie introduced us to his wife. I introduced Judy to them, and the four of us went into the dimly-lit coffee shop of the hotel where we could talk. There couldn't have been more than a few other couples in the room, so there was no noise or distraction.

We sat and talked late into the night, and I learned that Bernie and his wife, Arline, were residing in Phoenix, Arizona. On the same evening that he disappeared from our apartment in the Bronx, he and his girlfriend at that time (who I learned had been the receptionist in his office) had taken off in his 1957 Chevrolet. The car broke down in the desert and they somehow managed to get to Phoenix, where they made their home. Arline's two children from a previous marriage lived with them, but both had since grown up and moved out. Bernie and Arline got married, and we learned that we shared the same wedding anniversary.

My brother had an amazing success story to relate. He started out as a driver of a milk truck, and wound up purchasing the route. He built it up, adding the delivery of cheese and other dairy products, and started to save his money. With the accumulated profits, he invested in a cigar store. This was a natural since he had been the purchasing agent for a major cigar manufacturer before leaving New York. Since he had given no notice, he could not rely on a recommendation, and that is why he started from scratch at the milk company.

As the years progressed, he and his wife not only ran the tobacco shop, but invested in three more. The two children, his wife and he each had a store to operate. Bernie did the purchasing and the planning, and they enjoyed enough success to start a business of franchising similar stores. My brother was driven to prove himself, and he didn't stop there. For some strange reason, he bought a factory that was manufacturing ladies' pantsuits, which were very popular at the time. Not content with selling his wares to specialty shops, he decided to open up retail outlets to distribute his own merchandise. Here too, when things got rolling, he started selling off the stores as franchised operations, but kept a couple for himself.

I was flabbergasted. I always knew my brother was intelligent, but he had a self-destructive side. As a teenager Bernie was a compulsive gambler. He indiscriminately bet on anything and was in debt more often than not. I cannot count the times he came home with a shiner or blood dripping down his face for failure to pay his gambling debts. Other times he came home in the middle of winter without a coat or without the watch he received for his bar mitzvah. As far as my folks were concerned, these articles were always misplaced or stolen. I knew very well that they were either lost in gambling or used to pay off a debt.

Bernie had a pleasant side as well. He was my big brother who fought my battles and took me to the movies. When he ran out of money, I would loan him enough to treat me, and expect him to pay me back! This never fazed him. It was a shame that he never applied himself constructively, as he even dropped out of school without attempting to get a college degree. After moving to Phoenix, however, he went on to earn a B.B.A. at night. As impressive as all this happened to be, and even though I was proud of what he had accomplished, I had a difficult time not letting on how much respect I lost for him when he walked out on his children.

Bernie left it to me to share the details of this reunion with our mother and sister. They proved to be even more forgiving than I was, and it did not take long before we enjoyed having him back as part of the family. Bernie made frequent buying trips to New York, so we did get to see him on a regular basis. I felt that his wife (who happened to be about fifteen years his senior, and far from attractive) was aloof and untrusting. She had the unfounded suspicion that her husband's restored family wanted a share in their financial success, but that was the farthest thing from the truth. It was simply difficult to warm up to this suspicious woman whom I inwardly thought to be a home-wrecker. In spite of any personal dislikes, none of us ventured to say a word. Arline obviously made my brother happy, and that was the most important thing to keep in mind.

That evening in the hotel coffee shop was spent learning mostly about what had taken place in my brother's life after his disappearance. At one point the conversation turned to what was happening in my life. After filling them in on my career and our son, I proceeded to let them know about my faith in Jesus. Although my brother never exhibited concern for spiritual matters, or Judaism in particular, he was appalled. Not only did he find this hard to believe, he expressed terrible disappointment that I could have fallen prey to what he was convinced was a cult. I can still see him shaking his head in disbelief and declaring that his opinion of me was considerably diminished.

Over the course of time we managed to maintain a cordial relationship, and as long as I didn't broach the topic of the Bible or Jesus, the warmth between us would return. Interestingly, if the subject did come up, he raised it, and I took as much advantage as possible to have him understand the truth of what I believed. These conversations were brief, but I think he realized that my faith in Jesus was not a lark, and that it was far from being a casual flirtation. My brother always had respect for me, and he inherently knew that whatever I did was undertaken with careful thought.

Perhaps some six months later something happened that led to an interesting admission on his part. I had left a good job where I was respected and made a decent living. The company that employed me was a manufacturer of artificial Christmas trees. Somehow, as my reverence for scripture grew, it bothered me to work for an outfit that perpetuated what I deemed to be a holiday bathed in paganism. I had always taught at Beth Yeshua that the glitz and pomp surrounding this commercial holiday overshadowed the true meaning of the life and death of Israel's Messiah. A baby did not save us, but rather the Savior Who was nailed to the Tree. It took the blood of Jesus to atone for our sins, and that message was often lost. Certainly there was no scriptural evidence that Christmas was the actual time of Jesus' birth.

Most of the customs surrounding the Christmas season have little to do with scripture. Buying presents for each other, often going into debt, was not my idea of appreciating the forgiveness wrought through Calvary. To make matters worse, the prophet Jeremiah (chapter 10) admonished Israel: "Thus saith the Lord, learn not the way of the heathen . . . for the customs of the people are vain; for one cutteth a tree out of the forest, the work of the hands of the workman with the ax. They deck it with silver and gold; they fasten it with nails and with hammers, that it move not." My association with a company that profited by encouraging the heathen practices that infiltrated the church made me uncomfortable, and I felt constrained to leave.*

*It should be noted that many of my dear friends observe Christmas and put up trees in their homes. I respect their right to celebrate as they see fit, and do not expect everybody to feel as I do. My personal conviction, however, influenced my decision to leave.

For a year I worked as the general manager of a company that manufactured 14K gold rings. Although I improved the workflow and implemented procedures that tightened controls over the flow of the gold and gemstones, my boss wasn't particularly fond of me. Primarily, she realized that I resented working Saturdays. (This, by the way, has nothing to do with religious conviction, since I well know that I am under grace, and not under the law of the old covenant.) The point was that my boss wanted people around, whether or not the workload required it. She came in every Saturday, so she expected the rest of management to do likewise. Ultimately, the clashes between us led to a parting of the ways, and I was out of work

When my brother learned that I was job-hunting, he urged me to come to Phoenix where I would be made his second in command. He trusted me implicitly, knew of my work ethic, and recognized that I had years of managerial experience. It would be a perfect match, and I would become a partner. He was shocked that I declined, and expressed his disappointment.

I took another position with a company that manufactured eyeglass frames, but I was not happy there. My brother knew of my discontent, and continued to ask that I reconsider his offer. After a number of refusals that assured him that I was not about to change my mind, he said that he would give me one of his stores to own and operate. My refusal to accept such a gracious offer floored him. He then told me that if I were reluctant to move to Arizona, he would build a store in New York for me. I was very touched by his generosity, and I knew that I owed him an explanation.

I proceeded to write a lengthy letter, first thanking him for being so considerate. Far from being ungrateful, however, I explained that by refusing a partnership, I was protecting his interests. Based upon the teaching of the Word of God, a believer is not to be unequally yoked with an unbeliever. This truth, as far as I was concerned, applies to the marital relationship and to business partners as well. I believed with all my heart that if I were to be a partner with an unsaved person, even a brother, God would not bless it. My breaking fellowship with God would impact not only my own walk, but it would also negatively impact his success due to his involvement with me.

My brother called me after receiving that letter, and he told me that he thought I was crazy. No one in his right mind would refuse such an offer. He would take all the risks, and I had nothing to lose. Nonetheless, he added that he was never so impressed with me as being a man of conviction. He said that, whereas he thought my faith in Jesus was weird, he realized that there was something much more profound taking place in my life which was beyond his understanding. His respect for me had been fully restored.

A few months after our original meeting, my brother advised me that he had a bout with cancer shortly before the time of our reconciliation. He lost a kidney in this battle, but was now in remission. In retrospect, I can't but wonder if this illness motivated Bernie to reach out to his family. Obviously, I will never know the answer, but a serious illness often brings us in touch with our mortality, so it is not unreasonable to suspect that it sparked his desire to seek out the family he had not seen for so many years.

I was grateful to hear that he was given a clean bill of health, but that joy was short-lived. A few months later it was discovered that the cancer had now spread to a bone in my brother's leg. He underwent a course of radiation therapy that seemed to be effective. My brother needed a cane to walk, but once again the dreaded disease appeared to be under control. This too did not last long, and we learned that other internal organs were now under attack. Since Sloan Kettering in New York has the reputation of being the premier hospital in treating cancer, Bernie and Arline came to New York for treatment.

During this difficult period I never lost hope, and I kept my brother in daily prayer. Having shared my concern with the Bible class resulted in more prayer support. Every time we came together, my extended family joined with me in seeking the Lord's mercy. More importantly, we prayed for my brother's salvation. Bernie knew of the prayers being offered in his behalf, but was indifferent to whatever I had to say in this regard. While he was not disrespectful, it was clear that he saw nothing to pin his hopes on. Bernie was a fighter, he had confidence in himself, and he said that he beat cancer before and would do so again.

After a course of chemotherapy taken at Sloan Kettering my brother and his wife returned to Phoenix. We spoke often, and from what he was telling me, he remained fully active in his businesses. In the ensuing weeks I detected something in his voice that told me otherwise, but this was merely speculation. The confirmation of my suspicions came when Bernie said that he would not be able to attend my son's *Bar Mitzvah*, to which he had been invited. At this point be had to confess that he was growing weaker, and was limited in his ability to get around.

It is painful writing this in spite of the fact that these events go back more than twenty years. Bernie grew weaker and weaker, and scoffed at my sharing the gospel with him. Towards the end he emphatically declared in defiance that he had lived without Jesus and he would die without Jesus. These words cut into my heart, and nothing I could say would change Bernie's attitude. He was convinced that death is nothing more than going to sleep forever, and Biblical references to the resurrection of the just and unjust were without foundation. Man, and not God, wrote the Bible, and man's need for hope caused him to believe in life after death.

My brother wanted to die at home and refused to be admitted to a hospital or hospice. A hospital bed with all necessary facilities was set up in his home. Arline would give him repeated injections of morphine to cope with the pain, but it became harder and harder to deal with all of her husband's needs. She gratefully accepted my sister's offer to come to Phoenix and assist. My sister, incidentally, was a medical technician with many years of experience. Thus she remained in Phoenix several months, even though it meant being separated from her own husband for this extended period.

My sister came back to New York when there was little more that could be done. The excruciating pain that wracked my brother's body required attaching an intravenous that constantly infused the morphine. As a result, my brother was seldom coherent or alert. When he was coherent, the pain was insufferable, so he ultimately begged that he be allowed to die. The end came quickly, and, to my grief, without my brother receiving Jesus as Lord and Savior.

My mother, sister and I made arrangements to fly to Arizona for the funeral. The Jewish period of mourning *(shiva)* is normally one week, and it is customary for the immediate family to spend that week together as a means of comfort and support. My sister-in-law was glad to put us all up in her home, and the bonding that ensued is a tribute to efficacy of the custom observed by Jews for centuries. There were times of trial as well, but I'll get to that in a moment.

Since we came from an orthodox background, I wanted to respect my family's desire to maintain tradition. Even though I am free from the law, as a believer, it was important to show my mother and sister, as well as my sister-in-law, that my respect for Judaism had not diminished. For example, it's the custom that children recite the mourner's *kaddish* (prayer for the deceased) three times daily. Since my brother had abandoned his son, there was no one to fulfill this requirement. Under such circumstances you have the option to pay someone to recite the *kaddish* daily with a *minion* (quorum often required to pray in the synagogue) for the eleven-month period which ended when the memorial stone would be erected at the cemetery. I chose to say *kaddish* for the eleven months, rather than delegating this tradition to a stranger.

My first concern after the funeral was to acquire the low stools that the mourners were to sit on for the week of *shiva*. These are usually provided by the funeral home, but they did not have any. (Sitting on a low stool of wood or cardboard is an expression of humility during mourning.) I tried calling a number of funeral homes in the area, as well as all the synagogues that were listed in the local directory. There were none to be had, and I realized that Phoenix is a far cry from New York, which has a larger Jewish community than all of Israel. We had to improvise by sitting on hassocks or the floor.

I asked my sister-in-law where the closest orthodox synagogue was, and she gave me directions so that I could join a *minion* for the recitation of the *kaddish*. Not only did the synagogue not have a *minion*, they had services only on Friday evenings and *Shabbat* (Saturday service). It was apparent that my sister-in-law had no concept of orthodoxy. In fact, when I finally got to service, it was so ultraliberal that the *"rabbi"* was a woman. In New York we have come to take it for granted that there are at least ten men for prayer services, but this is not the case outside of New York. It brought to mind the time that my father had passed away and I was stationed at Fort Dix, New Jersey. I frequently had to drive to Philadelphia to find a synagogue with the required ten-man minimum.

A short time before my brother's death, I went to work for a watch manufacturing company owned and operated by an orthodox Jew who was a Holocaust survivor. Many of the employees were fellow survivors, and there was a large representation of all denominations employed by this privately-held corporation. They ran from various sects of *Chasidim* (ultra-orthodox), to neo-orthodox, like the members of the Young Israel community, to conservative and reformed Jews. Several of my coworkers were ordained rabbis. It was a real blessing having this mix, as I never had a problem finding a *minion* during the day. I still work for this company, and they continue to have a daily *minion* for the employees who are observant. Orthodox Jews pray three times daily, which includes *Shacris* (the morning service), *Mincha* (prior to sundown) and *Maariv* (the evening prayers).

My sister-in-law's son and daughter would often come over in the evenings to visit with us during the week of *shiva*. I didn't get to know the son too well, but I did spend some quality time with the daughter and her husband. The daughter had married a gentile, and I was led of the Lord to share my faith with them, explaining that in Jesus, Jew and gentile become one. Their faces lit up as I was speaking, and excitedly asked if I were born again. As it turned out, they were, too.

It immediately crossed my mind that since they had such a good relationship with my brother, they must have had ample opportunity to share their faith with him. It shocked me to learn that the subject was never brought up. Rather, they feared incurring the wrath of my brother and his wife, and kept their beliefs to themselves. The young man who was married to my sister-in-law's daughter had been raised a Christian, and had beautiful Christian parents whom I had an opportunity to meet. It never occurred to any of them that an unsaved soul goes to hell, and that they were grossly remiss in not witnessing to Bernie and Arline.

On another occasion I was able to spend some time with a housekeeper who had been in my sister-in-law's employ for many years. She was very close to the family, and it turned out that she, too, was born again. Of course, I was excited that she must have had the chance to speak to my brother about salvation. As was the case with Arline's daughter, the maid feared to invoke my brother's wrath by bringing up this subject. I often draw from these experiences when I speak in churches, reminding the congregations that the gospel is "to the Jew first". Though telling a Jew about Jesus may be difficult, and often uncomfortable, doesn't obedience to God's Word matter? Shouldn't the prospect of one of God's creatures going through eternity without Jesus override the possibility that someone might be upset with you?

One evening my sister-in-law walked into the kitchen where I was sharing with her daughter and her son-in-law. Overhearing the conversation about Jesus sent Arline into a rage. She felt that it was unconscionable that I would impose my beliefs on her family. She became so violent that I apologized for what she construed to be my abuse of her hospitality. I excused myself and went into the room where I had been staying. As I was packing to leave, rather than cause further distress, my mother came in and begged me to stay. I indicated that I had no intention to upset anyone, and that it would be better for me to go. My sister-in-law had lost the husband she loved, and if my presence made her uncomfortable, it would be better that I depart.

Arline and my mother convinced me that it would be preferable for me to stay, but that I was not to mention Jesus again. Although I was somewhat reluctant, I did what was best and promised to respect their wishes. Ironically, I learned later that my sister-in-law had a gut feeling that her daughter was embracing her husband's faith. On a number of occasions she attempted to reach them on a Sunday morning, and concluded that they were not home because they were attending church. (This brought to mind the similar suspicions mentioned by my mother-in-law with respect to her daughter and gentile son-in-law.) Apparently, it was better to avoid the topic rather than to confirm that your children attended a church.

Some of the things of which I write are of a personal nature, and I am not completely comfortable in disclosing character flaws or shortcomings that may be less than flattering. The intent of this book is to reveal the profound emotions that are stirred up by the mention of Jesus. Perhaps as the reader considers typical Jewish reaction to Christianity, it would encourage greater sensitivity in dealing with Jewish people. As mentioned before, if we understand the value of learning the traditions and customs of those approached on foreign mission fields, we should recognize that the same effort should be applied in reaching out to our Jewish brothers and sisters.

11

God Works In Mysterious Ways

In the Jewish faith it is customary to unveil a headstone at the gravesite eleven months following the funeral. Consequently, I arranged to fly back to Phoenix eleven months after my brother's passing. A strange thing happened on the trip down, but it is first necessary that I provide some background information to help explain this unusual event.

My brother was only forty-six years old when he passed away. It is difficult to lose a loved one at any age, but the loss of life for one so young is that much harder to deal with. Although my grandparents, uncles, cousins and even my father died around fifty years of age, I was not prepared to deal with this loss. Fortunately, my faith in God was unwavering, and with His help, I got on with my life. My mother and sister, who do not know the Lord, had a much more difficult time adjusting. I also had to consider the probability of my own abbreviated life span, but this was not a major concern since I know where I would spend eternity. Thus, I was more determined than ever to reach out to the unsaved.

It was around this time that a Jewish man, perhaps a year or two younger than I, started to attend the Friday night Bible study. A close friend of his, who was a gentile believer, brought him. Both of these men were music teachers in a high school on Long Island. Although the believer had shared his faith in Jesus, his knowledge of Judaism was limited, so he decided to introduce his friend and co-worker to a Jewish man who could better understand the Jewish mindset. This proved to be a wise move, for this unbeliever, Ron, and I hit it off immediately.

There were many unresolved issues in Ron's life which made it clear that he was searching for something. The problem was that he was emotionally incapable of putting his trust into God's hands. As is the case with so many particularly very bright and intellectually stimulated people, Ron wanted to be the master of his own destiny. He also had the typical reaction to perceiving Jesus as the Messiah of Israel. If it were true, his *bubby* and *zeida* (grandmother and grandfather) were in condemnation. "How could God consign such wonderful people to hell?" he inquired.

We spoke about the inherited sin nature, and the need for the atonement, but here, too, Ron balked at what he called Christian theology. In spite of my showing him the passages in the Old Testament that clearly speak of this, Ron refused to see its merit. Like so many, he had made up his mind that a loving God forgives, and does not allow good people to be sent to hell.

Ron may not have liked the implications of the teaching, but he did enjoy discussing scripture from a philosophical point of view. He saw me as an intellectual equal, and he was challenged by how I used the Word of God to support everything I taught. Since I had been through the gamut of emotions myself, I had no trouble understanding Ron's emotional rejection of what he could intellectually understand to be true. We often talked late into the evening and we began to meet outside of the Bible study to enjoy each other's company, and to explore the things of God.

Ron told me that he had originally been approached about putting his faith in Jesus by a gentile friend who lived in Des Moines, Iowa. That friend was the most gentle and loving person he had ever met, and they shared many things in common. In fact, this friend was also a music teacher. From the course of our conversations, it was apparent that this friend was Pentecostal, and he appealed to Ron's emotional side. The Pentecostal emphasis on God's love, mercy and forgiveness reinforced, in Ron's mind, that "good" people (by man's standards) did not wind up in outer darkness, alienated from God. Naturally, talk of the holiness and righteousness of God was more easily dismissed.

After several months Ron could not deny the logic of what I was teaching, but the conflict within remained an obstacle. Ron's relationship with his friend in Des Moines was over the telephone, and they spoke of what was being discussed in the Friday classes, as well as the relationship that developed between us outside of the class. It reached a point where Ron said one evening: "More than anything else in the world, I would like you (me) and Weston (the friend in Des Moines) to meet. Maybe then I would believe."

Since I never had occasion to go to Iowa, and Weston rarely came to New York, I dismissed this in my mind as being most unlikely. Besides, as it is written in Luke 16:31: "If they hear not Moses and the prophets, neither will they be persuaded, though one rose from the dead." Yet, something within me longed for a sign that would make Ron realize that God is very real and that His Word can be trusted implicitly. Over the course of the next couple of months Ron occasionally brought up Weston's name, but I did not give this conversation too much thought. As a realist, my main thrust is to stand pat on scripture, and to never forget that "faith cometh by hearing, and hearing by the Word of God".

There were a number of times that Ron told me that he believed what I taught was true, but at other times, he admitted that he had grave doubts. He was up and down like a yo-yo, and his sense of wellbeing was dependent on his circumstances at any given time. A large part of the problem was that Ron did not want to deal with the sin in his life, and he thought it unfair to quote the Bible as the authority for defining sin. Ron saw things as being relative, and if scripture pointed to something incompatible with his lifestyle, that scripture was subject to interpretation. Obviously, my "interpretation" was invalid if it made him uncomfortable.

By this time eleven months had passed since my brother lost his battle with cancer (the scheduled time for unveiling the headstone), and I booked a flight out of Kennedy Airport to go to Phoenix. Since there were no direct flights, I was to change in Dallas in order to get to Arizona. On the date of my departure I sat at the gate waiting to board, and learned that the flight was cancelled at the last minute. Fortunately, there was a flight headed to St. Louis where I could transfer to Phoenix, and it was getting ready to take off. I rushed to the gate and just made it. There was only one other person who had not boarded, and he apparently had a similar problem. He had been scheduled to fly into Dallas, but he could take a connecting flight to his destination.

Since we were the last two on board, we were seated together. I wanted to engage him in conversation so that I could share the gospel. Silently I prayed, and then tried to determine how to best begin. The gentleman took some sheet music from his attaché case, so I used that as an opening. "You must be a musician," I said. He responded that he was a music teacher who had come to New York for a concert. He was now on his way back to Iowa. He then told me that his flight was cancelled and that is why he was on this plane headed to St. Louis. I looked him in the eye and said: "Your name is Weston (I included his last name as well)". With a look of disbelief, he acknowledged that I was correct.

"How can you possibly know who I am?" he exclaimed. The puzzled look on his face was understandable, and I very simply replied that God revealed it to me. I added that we had a friend in common who told me about him, and that the name of that person was Ron. Weston continued to stare in amazement, and he asked who I was. Before I could respond, however, his face lit up and he said: "You must be Martin Fromm. Ron told me about you. In fact, it was his fondest wish that I would meet you."

The trip into St. Louis ended much too quickly. We had a wonderful time sharing with each other and relating experiences concerning our mutual friend. Both of us saw the hand of God in this predestined meeting, and we excitedly talked of how Ron would respond to learning that his wish had been granted. Imagine, even if we had known each other, what would be the likelihood that we would be seated next to each other? How much less likely when you realize that neither of us would have booked reservations into St. Louis!

Convinced that this was so unlikely, and figuring it would be next-to-impossible to convince Ron as to what had taken place, I asked Weston to give me something to substantiate this meeting. He had an issue of *Time Magazine* with the preprinted name and address label, and he handed it to me to show to Ron. I couldn't wait to see the look on Ron's face when we met next.

That Friday evening I struggled to hide my excitement, and then I casually made reference to a gentleman I met on my flight to Arizona. Handing Ron the magazine that Weston gave me, I remarked that the man I met requested that I give this to him. Spotting the address label, Ron's jaw dropped open in disbelief. "Where did you get this?" he asked. Although I filled Ron in on all the details, he was flabbergasted and kept saying it wasn't possible. The look on his face was everything that I had anticipated, and then I said, "<u>Now</u>, will you believe?"

I wish that I could tell you that Ron fell to his knees and asked Jesus to come into his heart. I wish that I could add that Ron's life straightened out at this point, and that he found the peace he had been seeking. Unfortunately, I'd be lying if I told you this. Ron did not make a profession of faith, nor did he find peace of mind. In the ensuing years he did claim to believe, but he would tell me on other occasions that he did not have faith in God. He continued to vacillate as long as I knew him, and life continued to be a struggle. Ron learned much from the classes, and did a lot of reading on his own. In spite of this, he could not reach the point where he put his life completely into God's hands. Sadly, he suffered physically and emotionally, unwilling to let Jesus take over. I'm fairly certain that Ron knew full well that Jesus is Lord, but he remained in rebellion because he continued to count the cost.

Ron ultimately left New York, and we are no longer in touch. Sometimes I think back to when he appeared to be so close to getting his life in order. There would be stretches when Ron would be cheerful and exuberant in his awareness of God. Then he would disappear from view for several months. When he sought me out, it was because he was floundering and he sorely needed a friend with whom he could speak openly, without having his confidence betrayed. He knew that I never judged him, and that I wouldn't hold back from telling him the truth. It took a lot for me to submit to Jesus, and I have never regretted that decision. I pray that Ron will learn this for himself.

12

Coping With Loss

I observed previously that the loss of a loved one is never easy. But, of all the losses that can be imagined, none can compare to the loss of a child. Common sense dictates that children anticipate a time that their parents will not be around. After all, based upon the age difference alone, it is normal for the parents to predecease their children. No parent, however, expects to outlive a child. Bearing this in mind, perhaps you can understand to some degree how hard my brother's death hit my mother.

She suffered deeply during my brother's illness, and I still can't forget how she would be sitting in the dark crying when I came home each day from work, following my father's untimely death. This added sadness claimed a heavy toll, and my mother was never the same. In spite of the years that have passed, there are memories of the time we spent in Phoenix that I can't forget. Most indelibly impressed in my mind was my mother's bitter cry at the funeral, "That's my baby, my firstborn!" My brother may have been forty-six, but he was still her baby.

My mom's health began to deteriorate following the burial of my brother. She was never the same, and it was not long before she was diagnosed as having angina. Her heart function was poor, and had advanced to a point where it was not operable. Only medication and a limited level of exertion would allow her to survive. Since I had already lost my father and brother without them coming to salvation, I was determined to do all within my power to help my mother to believe. She was a gentle and caring person who would avoid confrontation, and she never knowingly hurt anybody. My mother, sister and I always went to synagogue together, but my mother's faith was more cultural than spiritual.

At the outset my mother did not want me to talk about my faith in Jesus, but in later years she would listen on a limited basis. She tolerated my beliefs, but made it clear that she couldn't believe the way that I did. In order to provide a different perspective, I invited her to some of our holiday celebrations (Passover, Shavuos,

Succos), which she sometimes agreed to attend. She enjoyed the singing and informal prayer service, but most of all, she developed a real affinity for the people. My mother had to admit that she had never met such lovely individuals who were sincere and compassionate. She was particularly impressed by the gentile believers who demonstrated both a knowledge of and a love for the Jewish people and their customs.

Once in a while the Bible group held a retreat in upstate New York. Although my mother would not agree to go away for three or four days, she had no objection to my bringing her up for a day. While she did not join in the singing, she liked the music and the time of sharing. Listening to the messages was not exactly her fondest wish, but she endured them for my sake. My mother always complained that I was too laid back and that I didn't show enthusiasm for many things. There was no doubt in her mind, however, that Bible study and times together like this with other believers evoked a great sense of joy in me.

My mother was extremely limited in her activities, so she did not get out much unless I picked her up and drove her. I made it a practice to take her shopping every Saturday. If there was not a lot of shopping to do, my mother particularly enjoyed taking a drive with no destination in mind. This was a good time to look at the scenery and to talk. We both looked forward to these trips to nowhere. Her favorite time was when the leaves began to change color in the fall, and perhaps this helped reinforce her awareness of God's presence and handiwork.

When it got colder, it was next-to-impossible for my mother to leave the house. The wind and the cold inhibited her breathing, and she became a shut-in. In order to improve her quality of life, I decided that I would take her to Florida for the winter months. She loved Florida, and was thrilled that the temperate climate allowed her to spend time outdoors, but she missed her family. It became my practice to drive her (she was not allowed to fly) to Florida at the beginning of the winter season, and then pick her up for the trip north at the end of the season. I would usually get a *kuchelein* (a facility that offered a bedroom and kitchen privileges). Some converted hotels had a mini-kitchen in the room, and others offered a large room on the main floor that was sub-divided into many tiny kitchens. These proved to be the most inexpensive places to spend the winter.

Even though the *kuchelein* was much cheaper than most hotels and inns, it was costly. I felt it would be cheaper in the long run to purchase a condominium and to use it as a tax deduction. In this way, the net cost would make it a lot easier for me to afford. My dear friends in Florida, Ray and Lee Cohen, shopped around on my behalf, and I bought a place sight unseen. I was confident that they would find the best possible place for our needs, and that proved to be the case.

In order to finance this purchase, I approached my boss for a loan. His response was a real answer to prayer, and I marvel to this day as to how gracious he was in making this possible. God is good, and everything worked out beyond my wildest dreams. To make it all even better, it became possible for my believing friends in Florida to pick up my mother on Friday evenings to attend Ray's Bible studies. In spite of the fact that my mother was indifferent to the actual study, she enjoyed getting out and she developed a pleasant relationship with the people.

Sad to say, this did not last too long, for my mother passed away shortly thereafter. I never stopped praying for her salvation, and our congregations in New York and Florida were faithful in prayer as well. I have no assurance that my mother came to faith, and yet I do not dwell on what I do not know. I lost another dear and precious family member, but my faith in God sustains me. The only slight measure of hope came when I went to Florida to retrieve my mother's body and her personal effects: I found a Bible on her dresser with a bookmark, suggesting that she may have been searching. There is always the possibility that my mother made a decision that she never shared with me. I really do not know, but I'm convinced that God is holy and just, and that He makes no mistakes.

As I did for my father and brother, I proceeded to recite the mourner's *kaddish* three times daily for eleven months in my mother's memory. Once again I emphasize that I did not view this as necessary to accommodate Jewish law. I have always testified that coming to Jesus did not make me less of a Jew and that I didn't lose respect for our traditions. My twin sister and fellow employees were impressed by my desire to show this measure of respect for my family and up-bringing. Most importantly, I knew this is what my mother would have wanted.

13

It Is Well With My Soul

My twin sister and I had always been very close, but following the death of our mother, we drew even closer. We were the sole survivors of our immediate family, having lost our father, brother and now our mother. Prior to my mother's passing, my sister and her husband brought my mom to their house to live with them. They set her up in the basement where she had her own three-room apartment with a separate entrance. I made it a practice to come by weekly when my mother was alive, so I continued my Saturday visits whenever possible, but now I went to see my sister.

Fortunately, neither my sister nor I had any physical problems, because we both disdained going to see doctors. In spite of the fact that Doris (my sister) worked for doctors and hospitals most of her life, she sought medical attention only under extreme conditions. I was even worse. Prior to my son's birth in 1967 I contracted hepatitis, which required hospitalization for only the second time in my life. The first was when my tonsils and adenoids were removed as an infant. To the best of my recollection, that was the only time my sister was hospitalized as well, because our tonsils were taken out at the same time.

Doris may have seen a doctor on a few occasions, but not for anything serious. On the other hand, it was well over twenty years since I had seen the inside of a doctor's office. Ironically, I handle the administration of medical benefits for my office and deal with employee medical problems all the time. Yet, I would have to be dying before seeing a physician for my own needs. I am equally averse to taking any kind of medication, and doubt that I have taken more than three or four aspirins in my lifetime.

A few years ago I had no choice but to visit a doctor's office. While mowing the lawn I was attacked by bees and I was stung approximately twenty times. The pain and itching were so severe that I didn't sleep for two nights. By the third day I was concerned; not only was I in pain, but my arm was terribly swollen, and there was a blue line running up the arm towards my heart. Only then did I forego my stubbornness, and I resorted to calling the primary care physician on my health plan whom I had never met.

When I came to the doctor's office I was asked to fill out a questionnaire regarding my general health and family history. The doctor, who happened to be most pleasant, was incredulous that it had been so long since I had any medical attention. Since the male members of my family had passed on at such early ages, he assured me that I was less than prudent in not having periodic check-ups. With that, he put me in a little room, asked me to strip, and announced that I was not getting out of there until I was thoroughly examined.

The doctor didn't even ask me anything about the bee stings, and offered no comments or treatment in that regard. He wanted to check my heart and lungs and other assorted body parts. After checking every nook and cranny, he ordered x-rays and an EKG. His next question was when had I last had my prostate checked. I had no idea what that entailed, but learned quickly as he turned me over and inserted his finger in an area that had never been explored previously (and hopefully never again). Only when all of this was completed did the good doctor prescribe an antihistamine to alleviate the itching and swelling caused by the bee venom.

A few days later the doctor called my home and inquired as to why I did not call to find out the results of my tests. He had taken blood and urine, and now wanted me to be aware of the pathological findings. In brief, he indicated that I was in excellent health (for my age), and that my cholesterol, which had never been checked, was amazingly low. The lone drawback was that my HDL, the good cholesterol, was extremely below the norm. He added that there was nothing I could do about it, as it was hereditary. Fortunately, my low overall cholesterol compensated for the negative HDL level to some degree. Before hanging up, the doctor reminded me that I must come by for at least annual check-ups, and that I should consider having my colon checked.

It has been four or five years since that incident, and from time to time I receive reminder postcards from the doctor's office that it is time for my annual physical. As you may have guessed, these notices have been ignored. Only last week (as I write this chapter) the doctor's office called my home to find out if I have any intention of coming to see him. At this point, he may have figured out that he lost a patient.

I do not recommend that anybody be as cavalier as I am with

respect to examinations and check-ups. As foolish as it may be, I have such distaste for doctors and hospitals that it is hard for me to act differently. The Lord has blessed me with such good health that it boggles my mind. I do not take it for granted, and I give Him all the glory. I have already lasted longer than any of the males in my family, so I figure that my warranty has expired, and the Lord can have me whenever He chooses. I am not concerned about dying, for I will be with my Savior. My concern rather is that if I am to live, I don't wish to be sick, or to be a burden on anyone.

Since the body is the temple of the Holy Spirit, we have an obligation to take care of our bodies in which Jesus dwells. I am pretty careful of what I eat, and I walk and exercise regularly. In addition, I try to eat foods known to be of value in promoting good health, and I drink a lot of water, which is also recommended. As you can see, I do recognize that God is not obliged to keep me healthy simply because I'm saved. Each of us is responsible to do what is within our power to maintain good health. This includes getting sufficient rest, avoiding the use of drugs and tobacco, and not abusing the use of alcohol.

I have taught for years that we can stand on every promise that is written in God's Word, but we cannot presume upon Him to give us whatever we want. If there is no promise, there is no certainty. Those who preach "name it and claim it" are off-base, as far as I'm concerned. We're not guaranteed health or wealth, but we do know that "God shall meet all your need according to His riches in glory by Messiah Jesus" (Philippians 4:19).

This brings me back to my sister who, similar to me, enjoyed years of excellent health. Then one day she had a pain in her leg that was quite persistent and which inhibited her walking. The previous day, or perhaps two days prior, she and her husband were moving a piece of furniture. Doris figured that she must have strained her thigh in the process and did not give it much thought. However, the pain did not go away, and, if anything, it grew more severe. Weeks went by and she was increasingly uncomfortable. Typically, Doris did not seek medical assistance.

It reached a point that negotiating the steps in her colonial-style home was becoming increasingly difficult, so Doris started sleeping on a sofa in the downstairs living room. Both her husband and I told her that she should look into this matter, as she may have put something out of joint, and perhaps she should use an ace bandage. I told her that she was a real *ochshun* (stubborn), but Doris laughingly dismissed this, reminding me of the times I wouldn't go to a doctor for my sprains and strains. There were several times over the years that I was wrestling with my son and probably broke a rib or toe, but learned to live with the pain. Doris had advised me to get medical attention, but I ignored her as she now ignored my pleas.

Finally, the pain became severe enough to convince my sister to have x-rays taken. Imagine my shock when she called to tell me that she had been diagnosed with cancer. How could this be? We were sure that the x-ray would simply reveal a strained ligament, certainly not this dreaded disease that was responsible for claiming the life of our brother. All I could do was fall to my knees and pray. After the initial shock, I felt reassured that all would be OK.

Doris had access to the finest doctors. Ironically, the doctor for whom she worked was currently battling cancer, and was undergoing a course of chemotherapy. This doctor put Doris in touch with his oncologist, and we were reassured that the condition was treatable. After running a battery of tests, it was decided to give Doris a series of radiation treatments to reduce the tumor. Unfortunately, a lot of damage had been done already, and the femur (the bone between the pelvis and knee) was on the verge of snapping. A steel rod had to be implanted as reinforcement. Nonetheless, the radiation did its job, and Doris, with the exception of walking with a cane for support, was as good as new. Along with those in my Bible class who were praying for my sister, we praised God.

Approximately six weeks later, Doris was not feeling quite up to par, and they ran more tests. This time she was told that the cancer was in her lung. I was devastated, and could not believe my ears. Once again I brought this before the Lord, and called all my believing friends to keep Doris in prayer along with me. We also made it a practice to pray for her salvation as well. Doris knew of these prayers, but she had no desire to discuss getting saved. She expressed gratitude for the prayers, but wanted no intrusion on her personal beliefs.

After a brief stint in the hospital and what was described as a successful course of chemotherapy, Doris was able to return to work. I visited more frequently, always looking for the opportunity to remind her about Jesus. Naturally, I was tactful, and I wouldn't jam this down her throat. Doris was well aware of my faith, and had heard many, many times how I knew that Jesus is the Messiah the

Jewish people were to look for.

Within months the pain came back, but this time the cancer was spreading to a number of internal organs. Before long Doris was back in the hospital, but we never lost hope. Somehow I was convinced that my wonderful and merciful God would not deprive me of my only surviving relative. I never stopped praying, but I never stopped believing that this too would come to pass. But Doris grew progressively worse, and she was in constant pain.

Every night after work I would go to the Bronx to visit my sister in the hospital. She continued to lose weight and grow weaker. Sometimes it was too difficult for her to talk, so we just sat together in silence. I tried to be upbeat and comforting, and it took all my resources not to break down in her presence. I marvel that her husband, who does not know the Lord, remained so comforting and reassuring during those dark days. It reached a point that I was totally overwhelmed. My Lord had blessed me so many times, and now I had lost the assurance that comforted me. I began to entertain foolish thoughts and react like God owed me more than this. Life was unfair and futile; nothing made any sense –especially losing my twin.

I started taking long walks during which time I spoke to God. He used these times to turn my attention to scripture. He pointed out the lives of His saints; men like Moses, David, Joseph and Daniel who suffered without complaint. Though severely tested, they endured and continued to exhibit unwavering trust in the Lord. The trials of Jesus were brought to mind as well, and I knew that I was deep in sin. How could I not trust the One Who died on Calvary's tree to give me eternal life? I begged for forgiveness, and the peace (that surpasses understanding) returned.

During my sister's illness I did a lot of praying and a lot of reflecting. Looking back, I now realize that there was a lot of growth in my life when I came to understand that God owes us nothing. It is we who are indebted to Him. My biggest problem was seeking answers and blessings, not seeking Him and Him alone. This is all He has to reveal, and getting to know this is sufficient in itself. During the Passover *seder* Jewish people sing a song known as *Di-ei-nu* (It is sufficient). A number of rhetorical questions are raised to enumerate all that God had done for Israel (if He had only brought us out from bondage, if He had only given us the Sabbath, if He had only given us His law, etc). To each of these questions we sing a chorus repeating the single word, *Di-ei-nu*. Each act in itself would have been sufficient. How much more, then, are we to be grateful for His continuing mercy and goodness? The grace of God abounds, and we have no right to call the sovereign God to task. It is *chutzpah* (unmitigated gall) to think that He owes us an explanation.

My sister Doris was perhaps the most moral and decent human being whom I'd ever met who did not make an open profession of salvation. She lived by an incredible standard and had respect for all who crossed her path. It did not matter if you were male or female, white, black or green. Formal education was of no relevance as to the measure of a human being. She made friends from all walks of life, and maintained these friendships for years and years.

Doris originally graduated from a college and received a two-year degree in medical assisting. In spite of the fact that she was making a good living, she wanted to learn even more. Doris returned to school to receive a bachelor's degree and didn't stop there. If there was something more to be known that would make her a better person or better in her profession, she wanted to find out.

My sister became the president of a medical assistants' association, even though she was basically shy. It meant having to preside at meetings and training newcomers to the profession. Helping others was very important to her, so she took on increased responsibility in spite of her shyness and an already busy schedule.

Doris did not consider herself to be religious, but she lived by a standard that put others to shame. She would never dream of telling an untruth, nor would she consciously offend someone. She was very unassuming and she didn't quite understand the scope of her accomplishments. I made it a practice to go to synagogue with her on the High Holy Days, as she would not travel in violation of Jewish law. I fasted with her on Yom Kippor (The Day of Atonement), because I wanted her to know that I respected her customs. In fact, over the years of attending the same little synagogue, the people greeted me by her last name, thinking I was her husband. Doris' husband was not observant and never went to *shul*, so they had no idea what her husband looked like. My sister and I always laughed about this understandable mistake.

As I considered all that Doris' life meant to me, I wanted to leave her a kind of legacy. God had put it upon my heart during the last days of her terminal illness to write a book. That book which presents the Jewishness of Jesus from an Old Testament perspective is dedicated to her memory. I pray that that book will be used of the Lord to help Jewish people to find answers to many of the questions that we share in common. As I feel similarly led to write this account of my journey to faith, I pray once again that it will be used of God for His purpose. At the very least, I would want the reader to know that with all that has taken place, it is well with my soul. May my experiences help you come to know the same sense of peace.

14

The Conclusion Of The Matter

The book of Ecclesiastes, written by the wisest man who ever lived, reveals Solomon's search for happiness and peace of mind. There was nothing he didn't try, and considering the extent of resources available to a man of his wealth and power, he had it all. In spite of this, his frustration with the fleeting and transitory rewards reaped from the scope of his endeavors is apparent. All these acquisitions, in Solomon's own words, were vanity, and they resulted in vexation of spirit. It was only after exploring all these means of finding lasting satisfaction that Solomon advised (Ecclesiastes 12:13), "Let us hear the conclusion of the whole matter: fear God, and keep His commandments: for this is the whole duty of man." Borrowing this thought from the one who epitomizes wisdom, I come to the conclusion of this book.

From the outset I confessed that I struggled with the concept of writing what is in effect an autobiography. It is egotistical to think that my life is so interesting, or of such importance, that it warrants being recorded for posterity. Obviously, this is the farthest thing from the truth. My reason stems from the desire to reach out in a meaningful way on two levels. Both of these motivating factors arose as a consequence of my previous book, that was a much more scholarly approach to faith in Jesus. Many who read that book encouraged me to reveal my personal testimony to better understand how my journey to faith brought me to that point. Hopefully, unbelieving Jewish people who are not willing or capable of dealing with the profound and technical aspects of scripture will respond to the human approach.

Since my struggle and emotional turmoil are far from unusual, perhaps some would be inspired to investigate further by identifying with my experiences. Equally important is the reaction of gentile unbelievers who do not comprehend the range of emotions that create such a struggle within the breast of a Jew. I have always deemed it important to bring this understanding to the non-Jewish believer, for they are the ones who will be most instrumental in bringing Jewish people to faith. According to scripture, they are the means through whom the Jew will be provoked to emulation.

God alone has the power to save, so it is easy to say that in the scheme of things, whatever I do is of little consequence. On the other hand, let us remember that God chooses to work through His people, so it would be foolish to ignore the role we have been given to play. A single person can have an everlasting impact upon others. Look what one individual, Jesus, accomplished in the flesh! Nothing will ever be the same because of one solitary Person. We cannot negate the subsequent impact resulting from a handful of apostles who, according to the Word of God, turned the world upside down. Each of us must ask, as did Mordecai in the Book of Esther, "Who knoweth whether thou art come to the kingdom for such a time as this?" (4:14).

Whenever I prepare a study or a message, I ponder what can be said to make a difference. How do I stir up a desire to seek God, to search the scriptures, to look for answers? Even now I sit and wrack my brain to come up with a final thought that would touch someone's heart. I do not delude myself into thinking that I have the answers, but God's Word does, and this book will have served a purpose if some will have a renewed desire to become better acquainted with holy writ.

For too many, the Bible is a book of do's and don'ts; thou shalt not do this, or one must do that. I pray that others will learn as did I that it is so much more. The Bible is to be understood as the last will and testament of the Lord Jesus. If a rich uncle died and left you an inheritance, you no doubt would be front and center at the reading of the will. Well, this is the testament (covenant) of the Possessor of all wealth, and you can learn of your inheritance as a joint heir with Messiah, by searching the scriptures. In so doing you will realize that it is through this Book alone that we learn the mind of God. He so intimately identifies with His creation that He reveals His heart and mind within the covers of this Book. Only then can God be perceived as more than the Creator, Savior, sovereign King of kings, but as our Daddy, our heavenly Father.

This magnificent treasure that we call the Bible does not stop there. It goes on to be the mirror of the soul. As we open up the pages and read, we learn about our nature. Through the lives of those who preceded us and the words of the prophets, we begin to understand the sin nature and the wretchedness of man without God. A greater appreciation of God's plan for humanity, and the lengths to which He went to effect reconciliation, begins to unfold. God's mercy and grace takes root within, and we learn to respond out of love. The law, we are told, came by Moses, but grace and truth by Jesus. It is only then that we see past the rules and rigidity of law and live with hope instead of condemnation.

How encouraging to open the pages of our wonderful Bible and to gain assurance from such passages as Jeremiah 29:11: "For I know the thoughts that I think toward you, saith the Lord, thoughts of peace, and not of evil, to give you an expected end." Only through the knowledge of God's love and mercy do we begin to realize that we have hope and expectation; we can look forward to a glorious future, but it is based upon God's grace, and contingent upon our obedience. Sin will always be punished and obedience rewarded.

The best measure of truth is to look at the world around us. Pick up your daily newspaper; listen to the news on radio or television; read the periodicals and magazines. For six thousand years we have been making monumental advances in technology, and new discoveries are announced daily in just about every field of endeavor. But has human nature improved one iota? If anything, conditions grow increasingly worse, and that overshadows the gains that have been made. The Bible tells us that in the last days evil will be called good, and good, evil. We read how what was once a sublime human nature before the fall is to evolve into vile, self-serving, slanderous, covenant-breaking, egotistical hordes of reprobates.

Those of us who know the Word of God sit by and allow the wretched behavior to continue. The vocal ones who are willing to compromise with sin and accommodate ungodly behavior under the guise of love have sold us a bill of goods. Mistaking the true meaning of love, and ignoring the standard set by God, the bar continues to be lowered all the time. What happened to loving the sinner and hating the sin? At what point do we become so desensitized that we ignore the righteousness and holiness of God? Situation ethics and hedonism prevail because we no longer make distinctions between expediency and what is truly acceptable by God's standards. We refuse to admit that there are absolutes and that anything less is man's desire to avoid rocking the boat.

Compromise is a way of life, and, by contrast, standing firm is now called intransigence. We are frightened by the labels given to us by the unregenerate, and we back down from convictions to demonstrate our mistaken sense of sympathy for others. It has become easier to accept same-sex unions rather than being called a homophobe. It is easier to justify euthanasia and abortion than to call it murder. The popular theme is to aver that we have the right to do with our bodies as we please, ignoring the fact that scripture declares that we have been bought with a price, and that God alone has the right to tell us how this body is to be used.

We accept the most disgusting and profane language on television and in the movies. Displays of nudity have become commonplace, and believers have stooped to speaking and dressing in ways that make it impossible to tell them apart from the ungodly. By experimenting with cloning and embryonic stem cells we reduce human life to nothing more than resources. Ironically, more concern is demonstrated for the preservation of endangered species of animals than for humans.

God has been removed from most aspects of our lives. Prayer, according to liberal thinkers, poses a greater threat than AIDS and venereal disease. The problem, we are told, is not licentious and perverse life styles, but a lack of condoms and sterile hypodermic needles. Every day we see the standards established by God's Word overturned to allow more permissiveness and perversity. The blatant disregard for God, family life and old-fashioned mores resulted in the downfall of the great cultures that preceded ours, and we remain blind to our inanity. Our once-great nation will topple like all the others unless we who know the truth stand up and be counted.

The Bible teaches that we pay a heavy price for the praise of the world. It costs us the loss of fellowship with God. Without allowing our Lord to set the standard, we have no hope, and we fail to live up to our calling as the salt of the earth and the light of the world. Jesus said that the Pharisees received their reward here on earth; they garnered the praise of men. It is tempting to become satisfied with earthly treasures, but the cost is prohibitive. The Scripture warns, "Love not the world, neither the things that are in the world. If any man love the world, the love of the Father is not in him. For all that is in the world, the lust of the eyes, and the pride of life is not of the Farther, but is of the world" (1 John 2:15-16).

It is written (Proverbs 23:23) that we are to "Buy the truth, and sell it not; also wisdom, and instruction, and understanding." Each passing day that we allow the standard to be set by other than the

Word of God, we have sold out. The soul of our once-great nation is the price that has been paid by indifference and accommodation. Through my poor efforts in revealing the journey I have taken, it is hoped that others will learn that truth must prevail over personal gain.

I have to believe that there are many fundamental, God-fearing churches that preach these truths and uphold Biblical standards. Unfortunately, I am not convinced that too many of these institutions are equally adept at combining this teaching with the Jewishness of scripture while revealing the harmony between the Old and New Testaments. Understanding the scriptures requires more than New Testament doctrine, and we must remember that a wealth of information was written by Jews for a Jewish audience. Realizing this enhances and enriches the study of the Word.

Gentile people grow up with an awareness of Jesus, and even the least religious among them generally winds up in a church for Easter or Christmas, or for a wedding or christening. Conversely, the unsaved Jew will not be found inside the church, nor would he be amenable to the words of Jesus. I hope that this book helps at the very least to recognize the obstacles confronting Jewish people. Since the Jew is not in the church where the gospel is presented, and the gospel is not presented in the synagogue, I see this as a role for Beth Yeshua and similar ministries.

When I was first saved, the practice of Jewish outreaches was to recommend that the new Jewish believers attend a fundamental church. Not too many who came out of traditional Jewish environments were comfortable doing this, and they wound up getting lost in the shuffle. It is one thing to deal with the intellect, and another to cater to the emotional needs. The churches were either insensitive or poorly prepared to recognize the obstacles to Jewish growth. Many had symbols and pictures that are offensive to the Jew, and there are some which teach from an anti-Semitic frame of reference. As I have had opportunities to speak at churches in the Long Island area, there is no doubt that all too often an anti-Semitic slant inadvertently results from traditional commentaries and Bible footnotes that have been mistakenly perpetuated for centuries. A good example is the remarks often made about the patriarch Jacob who is accused of being opportunistic, sneaky and deceptive, in spite of God's declarations in Numbers 23: "How shall I curse whom God hath not cursed? Or how shall I defy whom the Lord hath not defied? . . . He hath not beheld iniquity in Jacob, neither hath He seen perverseness in Israel."

The teaching of scripture is that God blessed Jacob (Israel), and this understanding is reinforced in the book of Micah, where it is declared, "Jacob have I loved." I have taught on this theme many times, and hundreds revealed to me after my speaking that they had always harbored bad thoughts about this great man of faith. It is not surprising when you consider that the greatest enemy of the Jews is Satan. When Jacob is discredited, it is so much easier to discredit his descendants and the Messiah who comes from his lineage. Jewish ministries are much better equipped to promote clearer understanding on this and similar subjects of controversy.

In providing a more comfortable environment for the Jew, and including teachings about Jewish life and holy days, etc., the role of the messianic outreach is not fulfilled if it ignores New Testament principles such as salvation by faith alone, sanctification and justification. Thus, no work is complete if it is not a congregation where Jew and gentile become one new creation in Messiah. I fear that some messianic synagogues have lost this direction and go too far in attempting to preserve the Jewish roots of Christianity.

The apostle Paul wrote that those who are weak in faith might not be able to enjoy the same liberty as those of us who have been set free. When I initially came to faith, I was keeping a kosher home, and I continued to do so for a while afterward. There came a time, however, that I saw no purpose served by this practice. The important thing is that I never told anyone else what to do, realizing that personal conviction is one matter, and imposing values on others is something else entirely. Those messianic works that set legalistic standards for the congregation do a disservice to their members.

My journey to faith, the *shlepp* from Moses to Jesus, is intended to help you understand the Jewish mindset, but in no way does it suggest that gentiles are to become Jews. Why should a gentile be made uncomfortable in a messianic environment that is as alien to him as the church is to the Jew? All congregations must keep Jesus in the forefront and promote harmony between Jew and gentile.

15

Postscript: A Rose By Any Other Name

N ow that my journey to faith in Jesus has been completed, one of the most frequently asked questions is, "What do you call yourself?" A variety of designations have been used by Jewish people who have come to faith. A short list includes Messianic Jew, Hebrew-Christian, Jewish-Christian, Born-Again Jew and Bible-Believing Jew. Some do not distinguish between Jew and Christian, so they identify themselves as Fundamentalists, Believers or, simply, Christians or Born-Again Christians (this is to set themselves apart from nominal Christianity). Regardless of what we call ourselves, it is of no consequence for two reasons. Firstly, words and names mean different things to different people, and secondly, no matter which name we prefer, we are what others perceive us to be. That would probably relegate me to being a "Jesus freak" or *meshummed* (traitor).

The world tries to put people into boxes because it's easier to deal with something once it has a label. The truth is that most things are more complex than the limitations circumscribed by definitions. Thus, I remind you that a rose by any other name will still smell as sweet. Be prepared to understand at the same time that in the eyes of those who have already made up their minds, no facts will dissuade them to the contrary, and no title alters that preconceived notion. Call me what you will, but please give me the opportunity to explain in greater detail.

For a time following my coming to the conclusion that Jesus is Israel's Messiah, I was very defensive about the reactions of my unsaved Jewish brethren. I have since learned that you can't stop people from thinking what they will, and that a defensive posture usually does more harm than good. A sense of humor goes a long way in defusing some issues and can open the door to more meaningful dialogue. The most important thing we can understand is that we come under a microscope when we live for the Lord, so actions are a better illustration of who we are than all the words we use.

Within the generally-accepted definition of Judaism we find those who are orthodox, conservative, reform and reconstructionist. Each of these sects may argue the degree of responsibility in keeping the *Torah* (law), but few will not admit that all of these denominations are Jewish. Ironically, even a non-religious Jew finds a place under the umbrella of Judaism, and this can include a professed atheist or an agnostic. The lone exception is a Jew who professes faith in Jesus. Most Jews, regardless of background, regard this as a contradiction in terms.

I read an article a while back which was written by a prominent spokesman for Judaism. He wrote about a student of his who was being tutored for his *Bar Mitzvah* (the confirmation of a Jew who becomes a "son of the commandment" at the age of thirteen). This lad was honest enough to admit that he did not believe in God, and that he felt this disqualified him from going forward with the *Bar Mitzvah* training. The rabbi assured the young man that this did not present a problem as long as he was a good Jew. I wonder, do you deem this to be as outlandish as I did? Presumably, believing in God is not as important as keeping the Law.

I believe the scriptures to be inspired of God and infallible. I believe that the scriptures teach about the coming of our Messiah, and that prophecy defines who He is and how He is to be recognized. Having placed my faith in this One Who meets the criteria renders me a traitor, but an atheist devoid of faith can be, according to this rabbi, a good Jew! When Rabbi Saul of Tarsus, better known as the apostle Paul, was brought up on charges before the council, he spoke most eloquently: "But this I confess unto thee, that after the way which they call heresy, so worship I the God of my fathers, believing all things which are written in the law and in the prophets. And have hope towards God which they themselves also allow, and there shall be a resurrection of the dead . . . " (Acts 24:14-15). I suppose this puts me in good company, whether it pleases my critics or not.

The most prominent sect of Judaism that promotes the importance of the role played by Israel's Messiah is the *Lubavitch*. This *Chassidic* group is based on Eastern Parkway in Brooklyn, New York. They are a zealous community and have captured national attention by emphasizing the need for Messiah and the importance of *mitzvot* (good deeds) that will allegedly usher in the messianic kingdom. In addition to broad radio advertising supplemented by newspaper ads, many of the sect drive automobiles sporting large posters of their leader, Menachem Schneerson, and signs or bumper stickers declaring "We want *Moshiach* (Messiah) now!"

Dressed in conservative garb, long black coats or jackets, large wide-brimmed hats, and traditional beards and *peyos* (side curls), the ever-active *Lubavitchers* walk the streets asking passers-by, *"Du beist a yid?"* (Are you Jewish?). Those who reply in the affirmative are whisked into *mitzvah* tanks or *mitzvah* mobiles (vans) where they can be shown how to *daven* (recite prayers). These fervent workers are to the Jewish community what the Jehovah's Witnesses are among the gentiles. They are steadfast in their commitment to promote the need for the Messiah to usher in holiness, peace and the restoration of the edenic existence. These stalwarts of faith are in whole-hearted agreement with those of us who believe messianic prophecy, drawing the line, of course, when it comes to seeing Jesus as the fulfillment.

About seven years ago, their beloved *rebbe* Schneerson passed away, but a faithful remnant maintains a vigil at the gravesite in expectation of his resurrection. What amazes me most is that sincere Jewish people enthusiastically embrace the teaching of a mere mortal (admittedly brilliant, charismatic, moral and spellbinding) who does not match the scriptural description, while taking bitter exception to the claims of Jesus. For instance, the Messiah was to be born in Bethlehem, with his lineage traceable to King David through the tribe of Judah. Menachem Schneerson never set foot in Israel! Jesus came before the destruction of the temple, where the genealogy records were maintained, so that His pedigree could be established. Since the destruction of the temple, it is no longer possible to trace one's lineage.

Misplaced zeal and enthusiasm garners rewards and praise in most Jewish circles, as long as their traditions are not violated. Conversely, contempt and disdain are the order of the day for the earnest believer who stands on scripture when tradition is challenged. It is often joked that if you were to ask two Jews a question, you would wind up with three opinions. The one area where there is unanimity is in declaring that a Jew who believes in Jesus can no longer be considered Jewish.

Once in a while, some more open-minded Jewish people will probe a little further before dismissing my beliefs. They contend that my professing to be Jewish would make more sense if I were observant, referring to the laws of *kashruth* (kosher dietary laws) and *shabbat* (sabbath-keeping). "If you call yourself a Jew," they say, "how do you justify not keeping the Mosaic law?" For those willing to listen, I point to Jeremiah 31, which speaks of the new covenant relationship that supersedes the old. Here it was prophesied that the days would come when the Lord would make a new covenant with Israel and Judah (not the one given at Sinai when He brought us out of Egypt, which we broke). The new covenant that replaces the law would be in our hearts, and other prophets confirm that we will receive a new heart and spirit to know the Lord. This covenant of grace supersedes the law of carnal commandments fulfilled by Jesus.

There is ample precedent in scripture to reveal God's ultimate intent for us to realize that salvation is based upon faith rather than works. It is written in Genesis that Abraham believed God, and it was accounted to him for righteousness, and Habakkuk (2:4) told us, "Behold, his soul which is lifted up is not upright in him; but the just shall live by his faith." Why, then, does my faith in God's Word and prophetic fulfillment disqualify me from being a Jew?

This is not meant to be a theological treatise, so I have no intention of pursuing this point. The question of what is a Jew has been debated for centuries and remains a source of disharmony in Israel today. We hear of arguments claiming that Jewishness hinges on matrilineal or patrilineal descent, and how converts can be deemed Jewish based upon the rabbinical standards acceptable to some, but denied by others. No agreement seems reachable when these factors alone are under consideration. How much more is the possibility of agreement rendered untenable by introducing Jesus into the mix?

Realizing that I will never satisfy all or most, I am content to know for myself what is a reasonable answer. This is found in God's Word as spoken by Paul in Romans 2:29: "But he is a Jew which is one inwardly; and circumcision is that of the heart, in the spirit, and not in the letter; whose praise is not of men, but of God." But I would like to ask your further indulgence as I put another spin on this issue. After all, the term, Jew, technically refers to the tribe of Judah, but it has become synonymous with all the tribes of Israel, or one who is a Hebrew.

Abraham was the first Hebrew, which is a name that comes from the word *eber* (to cross over). Abraham was told to leave his family and pagan customs to cross over, by implication to be in opposition to heathen ways and practice. He was *Ha Ivri* (the Hebrew, or the one who crossed over the physical Jordan, symbolizing the spiritual separation from the pagan customs and his past life). The blessings that resulted from his obedience to this call passed to Isaac and, in turn, to Jacob. Jacob, as we all know, was renamed Israel, with the declaration that he was a prince, or "one who prevailed with God". I see myself as a descendant of the patriarchs of Israel, trusting wholly and completely on the completed work of Israel's Messiah, King and God - the Lord Jesus. It is He alone Who justifies me, and it is His Name that I bear. If you want to call me a child of the King, that's OK with me, too.

ABOUT THE AUTHOR

Born and raised in the Bronx, NY, Martin Fromm attended De Witt Clinton High School, and then earned a BBA from the Bernard M. Baruch School of Business and Public Administration. He served in the U.S. Army in Orleans and Poitiers, France. As a Chaplain's Assistant to the Rabbi ministering to the Southeast sector, Martin was a liaison to the French Jewish community.

For the past thirty-four years, he has been teaching the scriptures throughout the United States, and conducting home Bible studies. In 1998 he authored *FOR UNTO US A SON IS GIVEN - A Close Look At The Biblical Foundation For The Messiahship Of Jesus*, copies of which may be ordered from Beth Yeshua, 364 Plainfield Avenue, Floral Park, NY, or from ammifp@aol.com.

Martin's primary goal is to promote understanding of the Jewish contribution in preparing, presenting and promulgating the Word of God.

Martin is the president of the American Messianic Mission, Inc., a Hebrew-Christian outreach and fellowship headquartered in Floral Park, New York.

He and Judy, his wife of forty years, reside in Bayside, NY.